Edited by

Matilda S. McIntire, M.D.

Professor of Pediatrics
Creighton University School of Medicine
Omaha, Nebraska

Carol R. Angle, M.D.

Professor of Pediatrics
University of Nebraska College of Medicine
Omaha, Nebraska

9 contributors

suicide attempts in children and youth

HARPER & ROW, PUBLISHERS

HAGERSTOWN
Cambridge
New York
Philadelphia
San Francisco
London
Mexico City
São Paulo
Sydney
1817

The authors and publisher have exerted every effort to ensure that drug selection and dosage set forth in this text are in accord with current recommendations and practice at the time of publication. However, in view of ongoing research, changes in government regulations, and the constant flow of information relating to drug therapy and drug reactions, the reader is urged to check the package insert for each drug for any change in indications and dosage and for added warnings and precautions. This is particularly important when the recommended agent is a new and/or infrequently employed drug.

Printed in the United States of America.
For information address Medical Department,
Harper & Row Publishers, Inc.,
2350 Virginia Avenue, Hagerstown, Maryland 21740.

Library of Congress Cataloging in Publication Data

Suicide attempts in children and youth.
Includes index.
1. Suicide. 2. Adolescent psychopathology.
3. Child psychopathology. I. McIntire, Matilda S.
II. Angle, Carol R. [DNLM: 1. Suicide—
In infancy and childhood. 2. Suicide—In adolescence.
HV6546 S948]
RJ506.S9S84 616.85′8445 80-10868
ISBN 0-06-141610-X

10 9 8 7 6 5 4 3 2 1

That our sons may be as plants grown up in their youth;
that our daughters may be as corner stones,
polished after the similitude of a palace. . . .

Psalm 144, verse 12

contents

contributors

CAROL R. ANGLE, M.D.

Chapter Two
Professor of Pediatrics
University of Nebraska College of Medicine
Omaha, Nebraska

JAMES A. DAVIS, M.D.

Chapter Three
Associate Professor of Psychiatry
University of Nebraska Medical Center
Chief of Liaison Services, Nebraska Psychiatric Institute
Omaha, Nebraska

JOHN Y. DONALDSON, M.D.

Chapter Three
Associate Professor of Psychiatry
University of Nebraska Medical Center
Clinical Director, Children's and Adolescent's Services
Nebraska Psychiatric Institute
Omaha, Nebraska

EMMETT M. KENNEY, M.D.

Chapter Six
Chairman and Associate Professor, Department of Psychiatry
Creighton University School of Medicine
Omaha, Nebraska

KENNETH J. KRAJEWSKI, M.D.

Chapter Six
Instructor, Department of Psychiatry
Creighton University School of Medicine
Omaha, Nebraska

WILLIAM A. LONG, JR., M.D.

Chapter Five
Private Practice of Adolescent Medicine
Jackson, Mississippi

FREDERICK H. LOVEJOY, JR., M.D.

Chapter Four
Associate Professor of Pediatrics
The Clinical Pharmacology/Toxicology Unit
The Children's Hospital Medical Center
Department of Pediatrics
Harvard Medical School
The Massachusetts Poison Control System
Boston, Massachusetts

MATILDA S. McINTIRE, M.D.

Chapter One
Professor of Pediatrics
Creighton University School of Medicine
Omaha, Nebraska

R. W. MORIARTY, M.D.

Chapter Seven
Associate Professor of Pediatrics
University of Pittsburgh School of Medicine
Director, Pittsburgh Poison Center
Director, National Poison Center Network
Pittsburgh, Pennsylvania

preface

During the past decade, suicide has increased from the fourth to the second leading cause of death in the 15 to 24 age group, with an increase in suicidal deaths from 4:100,000 in 1957 to 13.6:100,000 in 1977. In adolescents, the ratio of suicide attempts or gestures to completed suicides is estimated, from national data, to be at least 200 to 1, suggesting that over one million suicide attempts and gestures are made annually by American adolescents.

To health professionals, the magnitude of the problem and the frequency of the challenge to deal with adolescent suicidal behavior prompted a symposium on the epidemiology of suicide and suicide attempts in children, sponsored by the Section of Community Pediatrics of the American Academy of Pediatrics at their annual meeting in October, 1978.

The chapters of this review evolved from presentations at that symposium. The awesome national statistics are reviewed in the first chapter. Parenthetically, it is noted that homicide is numerically almost equal to suicide as a cause of death in ages 15 to 24 years. The emergence of these two forms of destructive behavior, suicide and homicide, as leading causes of adolescent mortality is a manifestation of psycho-socio perturbation that appears uniquely representative of this era.

The epidemiology and taxonomy of suicidal behavior as seen by poison control centers shows that self-destructive behavior after the age of six is almost never accidental. Accidental poisoning is a maturity related behavior that ceases abruptly at age five years and any such events in older children deserve careful examination.

A validated method for the evaluation of self-destructive behavior as seen in poison control centers and emergency rooms is presented in the form of a psychological biopsy that can be utilized by parahealth personnel. Application of this biopsy has been shown to be effective in triage, particularly in distinguishing subjects with high lethality of intent who are at risk for recurrent self-destructive behavior.

The duration of perturbation as revealed in the biopsy appears to be the reason for failure of current therapeutic programs. These children are predominantly from disturbed families long identified by multiple social agencies, and a plea is made for earlier intervention, particularly consideration of foster home placement for younger adolescents.

Going beyond the viewpoint of the front line health professional, Doctors Donaldson and Davis present the psychiatric techniques of interview, diagnosis, diagnostic nomenclature, risk assessment, and decisions concerning the level of therapeutic management.

The outpatient management of the suicidally oriented adolescent is presented by Dr. William Long, a private practitioner of adolescent medicine with extensive experience in the pleasure and pain of maintaining communication and supporting these adolescents through periods of what they perceive as overwhelming burdens.

Doctors Kenney and Krajewski discuss the legal and psychiatric management of the adolescent hospitalized because of suicidal behavior. They stress the importance of confronting the adolescents with their fantasies that suicide evokes remorse and pity, citing Corporal Bloom in "From Here to Eternity." Bloom shoots himself with the full expectation that the whole company will run in with expressions of affection and concern; in actuality the shot is met with expletives that Bloom has messed up the barracks again.

A succinct summation of the medical treatment for the most commonly ingested substances is presented by Dr. Lovejoy of the Massachusetts Poison Control System. Dr. Moriarity provides an additional view of suicide gestures as seen in poison control centers.

We are indebted to all the participants in this symposium and, for our own studies in the epidemiology of adolescent suicide, to our research assistant, Mrs. Marilyn Schlicht, and to our mentor and consultant in statistics, Dr. Richard Wikoff.

suicide attempts in children and youth

one
the epidemiology and taxonomy of suicide

Matilda S. McIntire

During the past decade, the abuse of drugs and toxic substances in children, particularly adolescents, had increased enormously. The unintentioned deaths, suicides, and other personal social problems left in the wake of this wave have necessitated massive antidrug and rehabilitative programs in every section of the United States.

Suicide has been studied and analyzed from many viewpoints ranging from that of primitive man to psychoanalysis. Here we view the current scene from the pediatric perspective presenting the epidemiology and taxonomy of suicide and self-poisoning as seen in poison control centers.

EPIDEMIOLOGY

Fatalities from suicide in children under the age of 15 are fortunately low, but in the age group 15–24 years old, suicidal deaths have increased from 4:100,000 in 1957 to 13.6:100,000 in 1977; suicide in this age group is now second only to accidents as a cause of death.[14] The modes of suicidal death as reported for 1975 show firearms, poisoning, and hanging to be the major causes of self-inflicted death in the age groups 5–14 and 15–24 (Fig. 1–1).[10]

Poisoning accounts for only 25 percent of the fatalities due to suicide under the age of 25, but it is by far the most common mode of suicide gesture. In adolescents, the ratio of suicide gestures to fatal events is estimated at anywhere from 16:1 to 200:1. In our own col-

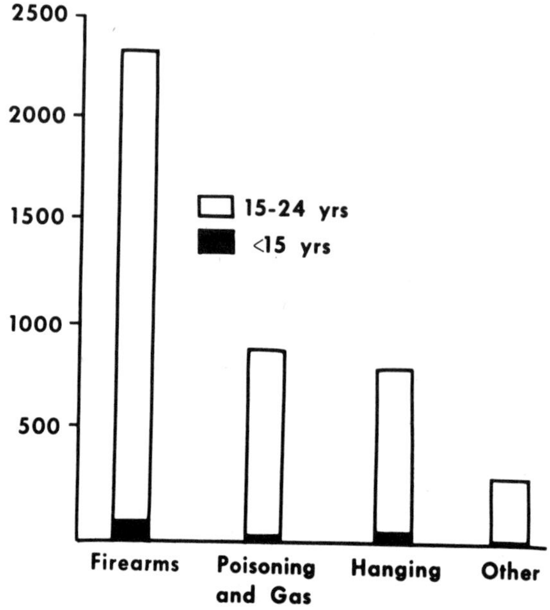

Fig. 1-1. Suicide Attempts in Children and Youth
Self-inflected deaths according to mode as cited in the U.S. Vital Statistics of 1975. There were nine deaths from poisoning and gas in the 5–14 age group, and 893 in the 15–24 age group. By 1977, the total deaths from all modes of suicide had increased from 170 to 190 in children 5–14 years of age, and from 4,736 to 5,565 in those 15–24 years of age. Suicide was second only to accidents as a cause of death.

laborative international survey of 1100 self-poisonings by children from ages 6–18, seen at 50 poison control centers, we found an incidence of 220 self-poisonings for every fatality.[3] It is in the emergency room that the primary care physician is most frequently confronted with self-destructive behavior.

Although mortality from self-poisoning is low, morbidity is high, and the frequency of symptoms supports the intentional characteristics of poisoning after the age of 5 years. Each year there are an estimated one million accidental ingestions of toxic substances by

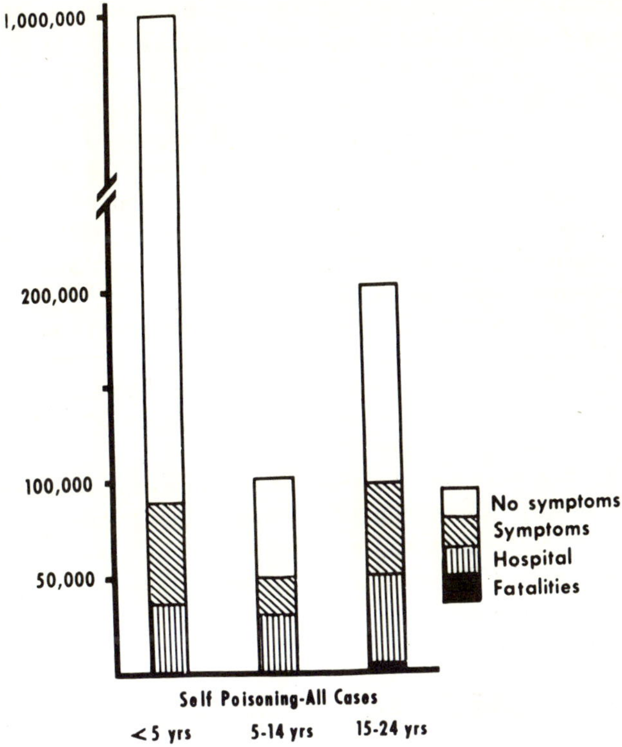

Fig. 1-2. Suicide Attempts in Children and Youth Self-poisoning, estimated at one million cases per year in children under 5 years of age, with an 8% incidence of symptoms and a 3% incidence of hospitalization. In poison control center cases of ages 5 and over, 1976, symptoms are recorded for 46% and 24% are hospitalized; these are extrapolated to the estimated number of cases for this age group. The 893 poisoning fatalities ages 15–24 in 1975, applied to the estimate of 150,000 events in this age group, suggest a fatality rate of 1:168.

children under the age of 5 years. The National Clearinghouse for Poison Control Centers reports that only 8 percent of these events evoke symptoms, and 3 percent require hospitalization.[11] In contrast, there are an estimated 100,000 self-poisonings annually in the 5–14 age group and 150,000 in the 15–24 age group, of which 46 percent cause symptoms and 24 percent require hospitalization (Fig. 1–2). Using the National Clearinghouse of Poison Control Centers Data Base of 150,000 events in ages 15–24, the 893 poisoning fatalities in this age group as reported in the U.S. Vital Statistics of 1975 represent an incidence of 1:168. It is important to note that this data is from poison control centers which typically see a younger age group than emergency rooms which care for acutely ill, older patients. With increasing age, the incidence of symptoms rises sharply and is the usual reason for medical contact.

Although any self-poisoning in a child over 5 years of age should be considered to have a major element of intent, the low incidence of fatalities (1:11,000 events in ages 5–14 years) suggests that the lethality of intent is minimal when compared with ages 15–24, where fatalities occur in 1:168 events.

It is ironic and tragic that many of the adolescent suicide deaths are unintentional—the victim did not really intend to die. For example, in our collaborative poison study, none of the deaths could be called intentional.[3] The adolescents were not victims of suicide but of pharmacologic roulette.

LETHALITY OF INTENT

The discrepancies in morbidity and mortality noted in the epidemiologic and demographic data concerning poisoning events in older children and adolescents demonstrate the need for a meaningful classification of the phenomena leading to the event similar to the taxonomy of suicide. A diagnosis of suicide attempt, as contrasted to a gesture or an affect reaction, implies both a lethality of intent and a mature concept of death as an irreversible cessation.

Lethality is defined by Shneidman as the probability of an individual's killing himself or herself in the immediate future.[12, 13] In addition to classifying all deaths as intentioned, subintentioned, and unintentioned (as opposed to the traditional, natural, accidental, suicidal, and homicidal), he has proposed the dimension of lethality to cut across the terms **attempted, threatened,** and **completed** suicide. Imputed lethality, ranging from high to absent, or scaled from

4 to 0, may be ascribed to the specific acts and life style of any individual.

High: The subject definitely wants to die and anticipates that his or her actions will result in death.

Medium: The individual is ambivalent, playing some partial, covert, or unconsicious role (as in drug abuse, foolhardiness, carelessness, or outright disregard of life-saving medical care).

Low: The subject plays some small but not insignificant role, such as the adolescent "inhalers" who have no conscious wish to die and yet are willing to take unknown risks.

Absent: No lethal intent.

In response to our emphasis on taxonomy of self-poisoning, the National Clearinghouse for Poison Control Centers instituted a classification of reported events as accidental, kicks or trips, and self-poisoning as a suicide gesture or suicidal attempt.[2] This can provide meaningful data, since cases reported to the National Clearinghouse are estimated at 10 percent of the national total seen at all poison control centers. Of the 147,277 poisonings in 1976 (of these 57,522 were over 5 years of age), a total of 40,402 cases were classified as intentional self-poisonings; of these, 16 percent were considered of suicidal intent and another 15 percent were classified as suicidal gestures.[11]

Adolescence is a time of great change, crisis, and pressure with a tendency for impulsive overreaction. This crisis–pressure behavior leads to manipulative and self-destructive behavior. Self-poisoning is rarely of high lethality, as demonstrated by Kessel in his Edinburgh study which concludes that at least 80 percent of self-poisonings are supported by the secure belief that death will not occur.[1] These individuals can go to the brink—but not fall off. They are not attempting suicide but rather are attempting to alter their life situation by playing the game of pharmacologic brinkmanship. Unfortunately, they do not know the toxicology of this pharmacologic game, so tragic results can ensue.

The best single correlate of imputed lethality is the probability of rescue. The probability of rescue is high when the mode of self-destructive behavior is of relatively low toxicity, but even behavior of high lethality is consistent with low lethality of intent if the victim anticipates intervention. The majority of adolescent self-poisonings, for example, occur in circumstances in which the victim will be found soon after the ingestions:

> A 16-year-old girl, living with her mother after her parents' divorce, did not get along with either her mother or her stepmother. However, she was fond of her father. After a fight with her mother she took a bottle of aspirin tablets and then promptly called her father. The father, having been through this scenario many times before, told the girl to drive herself to the hospital. She did this, was promptly treated, and returned home the same evening, with little done to modify the family dynamics except for a possibly beneficial insistence on self-reliance.
>
> A 13-year-old farm boy had an argument with his father and swallowed a relatively small amount of arsenic herbicide. Although the family found out about this almost immediately, they did not think the amount taken was significant and did not seek medical care until the boy was acutely ill. The boy died almost immediately after entering the hospital and the death was appropriately classified as unintentioned.

CONCEPT OF DEATH

It may be even more relevant to consider what the child and adolescent mean when considering death. The concept of death in childhood matures from believing it to be a sleep-like or reversible state, to a concept of personal continuation with cognizance of the world being left, then reaching the concept of spiritual continuation or total cessation. Shneidman had emphasized that suicide is an inappropriate diagnosis if the individual does not view death as permanent and irreversible.[12] It would seem that adolescents making suicide gestures would be less likely to view death as irreversible cessation. For this reason, we first investigated the maturation of the concept of death, its causes, imagery, and finality as expressed by 598 children, ages 5 to 18 years, in structured interviews held at a pediatric clinic and at three religious schools—Roman Catholic, Protestant, and Conservative Jewish (Table 1–1).[8]

Table 1-1. Structured Interview—Concept of Death

1–4. Age, sex, race, religion
5. Frequency of religious instruction (coded from 0 to daily)
6. Family status (coding includes intact family, loss or death of mother, loss or death of father)
7. Have you ever had a pet die?
8. What happened to the body after burial or disposal? (Coding includes fantasy, preserved forever, organic decomposition, disintegration to ashes or dust)
9. Do you think it will ever come back to life?
10. Do you think it will ever come back in a different form?
11. Do you think it knows you miss it?
12. Why do people die?

Acquaintance With Death

13. Did you ever know anyone who died? Who?
14. What did they die of?
15. Did you ever see a dead person?
16. Did you ever go to a funeral?
17. If you die, what happens to you? (Coded as Number 8)
18. Is dying like going to sleep? Can you wake up again?
19. Can people who die sometimes return to life?
20. If the body is dead, does a spirit or soul live on?
21. Can the spirit or soul think just as the living person did?
22. After a person dies, does he know what people on earth are doing?
23. When a person dies, does all life and thought end?
24. Are there times when you really wish you were dead?
25. What kind of things make you feel that way?
26. Which people would care most?
27. What does life mean to you? (Coded as simple pleasures, biosocial immortality, theologic, transcendental)

In this study, the "why" of death was most affected by socioeconomic status; death as due to violence was seen most often by the clinic children. Somewhat surprisingly, the imagery of what happens to the body after death was rarely terrifying, but more realism concerning organic decomposition was tolerated for pets than for self. In all groups, the young child up to age 5 or 6 had an immature concept and saw death as reversible. The grade-school child had an awareness of the permanent state, with a mature concept beginning to appear at age 11. By ages 13 to 16, 20 percent still thought that when dead they would be cognizant, 60 percent envisioned spiritual continuation, and 20 percent saw death as total cessation.

In response to the question, "Are there times when you *really* wish you were dead?," 238 (40%) of 598 children replied "occasionally," and 18 (3%) said "frequently," and were considered to have a possible suicidal ideation. The 18 children admitting a frequent death wish were over the age of 10 years, were more often Protestant (14/18), came from intact families, and received religious instruction at least once per week. Their concept of death was less naturalistic than that of the total group, with more fantasy of imagery (particularly reincarnation), and they were likely to believe in reversibility or cognizance for themselves after death.

In this part of the group, their formulation of the significance of life was less mature than that of the entire group and was focused on simple pleasures. This supports the concept that youthful integration of the prospect of death into the adolescent personality has profound implications for the individual's mastery of life. This sense of personal insignificance was evident in the frequency of their report that their feelings of a wish for death; were most often (10/18) precipitated by family arguments or fear of punishment and most often characterized by feelings of anger or sadness.

The professed concept of death, however mature, may obviously differ from the emotional need to believe in the unique immortality of self. In a subsequent investigation of the concept of death of 50 adolescents who attempted suicide, we found no difference between the maturity of their concept of death and that held by a control group matched for age, sex, religion, and socioeconomic status.[4, 5] The adolescent has a sense of personal immortality no matter what his or her stated concepts are, because during adolescence one's own death is so remote in time; one enjoys the invincibility of youth.

TAXONOMY AS SEEN IN POISON CONTROL CENTERS

To investigate the taxonomy of self-poisoning, a 1-year cooperative study was carried out at 50 poison control centers, 46 in the United States, two in Canada, and one each in Scotland and New Zealand.[3]

These poison control centers provided the demographic data on 1103 cases of self-poisoning in children aged 6 to 18. The sex distribution of patients between 6 and 10 (Fig. 1–3) showed a predominance of males even greater than that found for poisoning under age

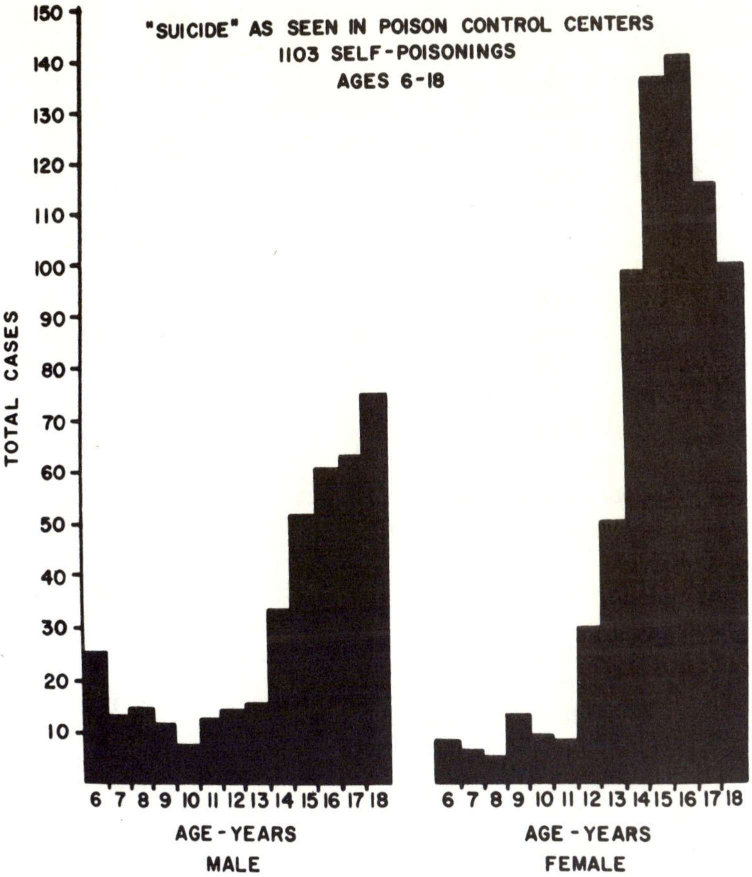

Fig. 1-3. Suicide Attempts in Children and Youth
Age and sex distribution of 1103 patients over 5 years of age as seen in poison control centers for self-poisoning in our early collaborative investigation of the problem. *(McIntire MS, Angle CR: The taxonomy of suicide as seen in poison control centers. Pediatr Clin of North Am 17:697–706, 1970; and from McIntire MS, Angle CR: "Suicide" as seen in poison control centers. Pediatrics 48:914–922, 1971.)*

5, and may represent cases of cognitive immaturity or persistence of male propensity for accidental injury. The sudden spurt of self-poisoning by adolescent girls at age 12, with a decrease after age 16, reflects earlier biologic maturation and subsequent social conflicts. In contrast, the events in males continued to increase at ages 17 and 18, and would seem to presage the known increase with age of male suicide.

Socioeconomic status based on the occupation of the head of the family correlated with the racial distribution. As age increased, Blacks accounted for a decreasing percentage. For Hispanics and American Indians, the peak incidence was among females, ages 14–16, with a subsequent decrease as shown in Table 1–2.

The older conflict between the sociologic and psychiatric evaluation of suicide has receded into a clinical approach that does not at-

Table 1-2. Race, Age, and Sex of 1103 Self-poisonings, Ages 6–18

Female (Age in years)	*White (%)*	*Black (%)*	*American Indian, Hispanic (%)*	*Other or not reported (%)*
6–10	59	39*	0	2
11–13	61	27*	8	4
14–16	64	22	11*	3
17–18	77†	13	4	6
Total Female	67	21	8	4
Male (Age in years)				
6–10	44	40†	6	10
11–13	60	33	2	5
14–16	76	13	5	6
17–18	85†	6	4	5
Total Male	72	18	4	6
Total, Male and Female	69	20	7	4

*$p<0.05$
†$p<0.005$
Analysis of the percent distributions by Chi-square tests shows an increase in Black girls aged 6–10 and 11–13, and an increase in Hispanic and American Indian girls aged 14–16. Among boys, there was a disproportionately high number of Blacks aged 6–10 and of Whites aged 17 and 18.

Table 1-3. "Accidental" Poisoning, Ages 6–18—History

Behavior disorder	10%	Chronic medical problems	2%
Character disorder	6%	Convulsive disorder	2%
"Loner"	5%	Brain damage	1%
School dropout	5%	Multiple problems	7%
Delinquency	4%	No significant problems	31%
Psychoneurosis	4%	No information	20%
Psychosis	2%		

Table 1-4. Age and Precipitating Stress

Age (years)	*Present (%)*	*Absent (%)*	*Not reported (%)*
6–10	42	37	21
11–13	73	14	13
14–16	78	7	15
17–18	81	6	13

tempt to fit patients into a rigid categorization of psychodynamics. The diversity of individual problems was apparent in the patients' past histories and in the precipitating events. Inquiry was made concerning significant psychosocial disruption: loner, school dropout, juvenile delinquent, a character or behavior disorder, brain damage (motor or mental), a convulsive disorder, psychoneurosis, psychosis, a significant or chronic mental disability or illness (Table 1–3). The 10 percent incidence of behavior disorders would support adolescent depression and suicide as late manifestations of an early antagonism between the parent and child.

A history of significant emotional stress at the time of poisoning was obtained from the majority of older patients interviewed and from 43 percent of the youngest age group (Table 1–4). These stressful situations were listed on the questionnaire as humiliation, punishment, sense of failure, romance problems, pregnancy, family problems, loss of parent or other significant relative, and "other difficulties." In the youngest age group, acts of overt aggression, hostility, and fear of retribution were the most common difficulties. This is the most transparent expression of suicide as hate. Of the girls 17 or 18-years-old, 30 percent had experience with marriage, (were married, separated, or widowed) or pregnancy (unwed mothers or unwed and pregnant). In boys, homosexuality was frequently reported. Precipitating stress revolved around the five P's: parents, peers, privation, punctured romance, and pregnancy.

Intent, meaning the deliberate attempt to poison oneself, was assessed by the poison control centers (Table 1–5). In children ages 6 to 10, 50 percent of poisonings are called unintentional, but this naive interpretation is not supported by behavioral data: the 6- to 10-year-old selects sedatives twice as frequently as the 4-year-old; at least 24 percent of such children are referred to behavior clinics; 26 percent have a history of past difficulties; 43 percent give a history of current precipitating stress factors. Only 8.6 percent of the 992 cases in patients ages 11 to 18 were considered "unintentional," and these usually involved errors with prescription drugs.

Table 1-5. Age and Diagnosis of Intent

Age (years)	*Intentional (%)*	*Subintentional (%)*	*Unintentional (%)*	*Unknown (%)*
6–10	13	19	50	18
11–13	53	23	16	9
14–16	64	21	7	7
17–18	67	17	8	7
Total	59	20	13	8

In making diagnosis of suicide attempt, the interviewers were asked to consider the question, "Did the subject mean to kill himself?" The frequency of diagnosis is shown in Table 1–6.

The diagnosis of a suicide attempt by an observer was related to:

1. Age
2. Drug use (i.e., a "kick" or "trip" was rarely called a suicide attempt)
3. The history of prior psychosocial disruption
4. Precipitating stress
5. Socioeconomic status. Significantly greater attention was given to the possibility of suicide attempt in patients from the upper socioeconomic group.

Table 1-6. Age and Diagnosis of Suicide Attempt

Age (years)	*Final diagnosis (%)*	*Considered not final (%)*	*Never considered (%)*	*Not reported (%)*
6–10	2	9	69*	20
11–13	20	29	42†	9
14–16	32	31	26	11
17–18	28	31	34	7
Total	26	29	35	10

* $p<0.05$
† $p<0.005$
The frequency of the diagnosis of suicide increases with age, but is considered and even diagnosed in children as young as 6 years.

This study was the first time an attempt had been made, on an international basis, to investigate the dynamics of "accidental" poisoning after 5 years of age. Considerable regional diversity was evident. Edinburgh, Scotland, for example, continuing in the clear distinction between gesture and attempt, did not label a single adolescent ingestion as a true suicide attempt. Our most important evidence here was that only 13 percent of poisoning at ages 6 and older were considered true accidents. The fact that intent was evident in 75 percent of the cases studied must redefine the concept of accidental poisoning in school-age children as young as 6 years of age.

The general classifications of toxic substances showed a distinctive pattern for each age group. Intent is suggested by the fact that 27 percent of 6- to 10-year-olds ingested sedatives, twice as frequently as did 4-year-olds. Young thrill-seekers favored alcohol and glue inhalation over other hallucinogens. Drug abuse tripled after age 13.

Death occurred in 5 patients, a mortality of 1:220 self-poisonings. In all cases it appeared that lethality of intent was extremely low, and death was the result of toxicologic mishap.

The results of this initial survey showed that self-poisoning in a child over 6 years of age is rarely accidental, and deserves inquiry by the health professional into the severity and chronicity of prior difficulties and disruptive events, the nature of the precipitating stress, and, most important, the motivation for the act. One needs to know what the child expects to happen physically as a result of the ingestion, and what life changes are expected. The actual self-poisoning may be the end stage of long-standing problems, or it may be an impulsive attempt to control interpersonal conflict by a child or adolescent who sees himself or herself as so unimportant that only acute behavior will merit attention.

EVALUATION—THE PSYCHOLOGICAL BIOPSY

Given the frequency of initial contact in the emergency room or poison control center, the emergency room physician is a valuable resource for the assessment of self-poisonings, suicide, gestures, and suicide attempts in children and adolescents. Systematic examination and evaluation of these adolescents present the opportunity to study suicidopathic behavior and drug abuse in its most transparent form. Having redefined the concept of poisoning in the older child as an intentional event, our next study was to investigate these children in depth. For this purpose we devised a structured interview and rating system called a "psychological biopsy," and established its validity when administered by health professionals of varying backgrounds.[6]

The interview is conducted as soon as the patient is no longer in danger. In the interim, the rescuers' view of both the immediate event and the past history should be obtained. The adolescent should be interviewed in a private room and assured that the information will not be used against him. It is essential to maintain confidentiality despite legal pressures and parental concern. The three general areas of inquiry are outlined in narrative form in Table 1–7.

The immediate circumstances, particularly information on the probability of rescue, are most useful in estimating the lethality of intent at the time of the self-destructive behavior. The actual event, however, is only one item in a long history of difficulties. The family history usually depicts great stress and strife. A history of multiple prior difficulties plus antisocial behavior usually indicates a low lethality of intent; rage has been channeled into rebellious rather than suicidal behavior. The exceptional history, in which family perturbation appears low or even absent, is often the first indication of a severe psychiatric disorder.

The "psychological biopsy" (Table 1–8) scores nine significant areas of evaluation. Scoring of these items is derived from the initial history supplement by additional questions as individual circum-

Table 1-7. Narrative Outline for Evaluation of Adolescent Suicidal Behavior

Narrative Outline of Event:
Tell me what happened. (**Actual lethality of event**) What time of day? What did you do then? Did you tell anyone? Did you think you would be found? How did they find out about it? (**Probability of rescue**) When did you first think about doing this? (**Premeditation**) Have you ever done anything like this in the past? Do you think you will do anything like it again?
Rating of Circumstantial Lethality:
0 None — 1–2 Low — 3–4–5 Medium — 7–8–9 High
Narrative Outline of Family and Interactions:
Tell me about the members of your family, their ages, where they live, how you get along with each. Do you think any of them uses too much alcohol or drugs? Have any of your family or close friends ever attempted suicide? Which people can you talk to when things go wrong? If you could make some changes in your life, what would you change?
Prior Difficulties, Symptoms, and Perturbation:
What medical problems have you had? Have you had any school problems? Repeat a class? Dropping out? Suspended? Have you had any trouble with the police? Any trouble because of alcohol or drugs? Ever run away from home? Has a doctor ever treated you for your nerves? Have you had many problems with your boyfriend or girlfriend? Your friends? Marriage problems?

stances indicate. The goals of the assessment are (1) diagnosis—"Is this really a suicide attempt?" and (2) definition of the nature and severity of perturbation.

The final item in the questionnaire, familial expectations and control, overlaps the ratings of stress and parental reaction. It is included as a separate item because of its critical relationship to adolescent behavior. In adolescents manifesting suicidal behavior, the pattern of familial control and demands is often at one extreme or the other. The dominant group of these adolescents comes from families characterized by indifference, low expectations, and sporadic control.[7] These young people are most inclined to act out their hostility and have frequent problems with the law. At the other extreme are those subjected to all-pervasive control and excessive expectations. Some children from this kind of family are incapable of rebellion

Table 1-8. Psychological Biopsy Questionnaire

Name: ____________ Age: ____ Sex: ____ Race: ______

Occupation, head of household: ______________

Lives with: __________ Address: ______________

Score each category as:

0	1–2	3–4–5	7–8–9	Score (0–9)
None	Low	Medium	High	______

1. Circumstantial lethality: (______)
   Probability of rescue ____; subject's impression of lethality ____; actual lethality ____; extent of planning ____; plans to repeat ____.

2. Prior self-destructive behavior: (______)
   One or more suicide attempts/gestures ____; suicidal preoccupation ____; "accidental" poisoning after age 6 ____; more than one accident/year requiring medical care ____; drug or alcohol use considered excessive by peer group ____; refuses or denies needs for health care ____.

3. Depression: (______)
   Loneliness, hopelessness, exhaustion ____; disorders of sleep ____; appetite ____; chronic illness ____.

4. Hostility: (______)
   Feelings of rage, anger, hostility, revenge ____; poor judgment, irresponsibility and impulsive acting out ____; overt belligerence, aggression, antisocial behavior ____.

5. Stress: (______)
   Chronicity and muliplicity of conflicts ____; broken or unsympathetic home ____; loss of parent, sibling, or significant other by death, divorce, or desertion ____; alcoholic or otherwise irresponsible parent(s) ____; threat of punishment, criminal prosecution, exposure ____; concern over homosexuality ____; other ____.

6. Reaction of parent or parent surrogate: (______)
   Helpless ____; indifferent ____; angry ____; punitive ____; vacillating ____; parent(s) alcoholic ____; other psychosocial difficulty ____.

7. Loss of communication: (______)
   Broken with one or both parents ____; with all adults ____; with most peers ____; all peers ____.

8. Lack of resources: (______)
   Lack of religious ties ____; lack of availability of professional help—counselor, etc. ____.

9. Parental expectations and control: (______)
   Subject feels parental demands or expectations beyond his capacity; feels a disappointment to parents ____; parents expect nothing from him ____; parent or surrogate demands review of friends, activities ____; refuses any discussion or negotiation of control ____; extreme indifference or neglect ____; vacillates from one extreme to other ____; expectations and degree of control divergent ____.

and have more severe psychiatric disorders. The extremes of parental reaction offer the caseworker or clinician some of the best opportunities for environmental change and supportive encouragement of the patient, helping him or her to recognize the nature of the oppression and rejection.

Our first study using this biopsy involved single interviews (conducted in the home by public health nurses) of 50 consecutive patients, ages 6–18, who had recently been treated at two poison control centers in Omaha; there were concurrent interviews of 50 controls matched for age, sex, socioeconomic and family status. The last was considered particularly important because of the high incidence of single parent, stepparent, and otherwise disrupted families.

Long-standing personal difficulties coupled with precipitating stress were found in almost all cases (Table 1–9). Thirty-two percent

Table 1-9. History, 50 Self-poisonings, Ages 6–17

History	*Subjects (%)*	*Controls (%)*
Prior mental health referral	32	2
Prior behavior problems	88	12
Prior suicide gestures	26	0

of the subjects, but none of the controls, had at least one prior referral to a mental health service. In contrast to 12 percent of the controls, 88 percent of the subjects had a past history of significant personal–social difficulties. The most frequent problems were immaturity (38 percent), dropping out of school (18 percent), being a loner (16 percent), having a behavior problem (16 percent), and delinquency (14 percent). Prior suicide gestures had been made by 26 percent of the subjects, but by none of the controls.

The following is a typical example of long-standing perturbation culminating in a precipitous action.

> An 18-year-old boy, whose mother was a housewife and whose stepfather was a laborer, was a school dropout and had a history of chronic ulcers. He stated he was a failure, had trouble with his girlfriend, and feared he might die of kidney disease

as did his brother. After his father was killed in an accident, his mother remarried and had three more children. At the time of the ingestion of tranquilizers and sleeping pills, his mother was filing for divorce. The youth said his mother was crazy but refused psychiatric help. He said his girlfriend was pregnant by him. "I'd had it—my life was a mess—I know what I am, and that's no good. I've thought about suicide many times and finally I really wanted to die." When asked what would be the best thing that could happen, he said, "Get married—then my suicide problem would go away." When asked about death, he answered "It's final, you finally have peace; I want to die, I've tried and will probably try again." Despite the irrationality of his belief that marriage would solve his problems, this boy was clearly asking for relief from these overwhelming circumstances.

The interview by the public health nurse almost always disclosed information not obtained at the hospital, and refined the diagnosis in 96 percent of the cases.

The diagnoses based on the psychological biopsy showed only two of 50 events in subjects ages 6–18 to be accidental: a 7-year-old girl followed a neighboring child's lead in filling a small swimming pool with gasoline and was then overcome by the fumes; a 12-year-old boy, maladjusted in many areas, put a lump of dry ice in his mouth on a dare.

Twenty-two percent of the events were considered intoxications. These were occasionally experimental or convivial in nature, but

Table 1-10. Diagnosis, 50 Self-poisonings, Ages 6–17

Hospital Diagnosis	
Accident	58%
Suicide attempt	42%
Biopsy Diagnosis	
Accident	4%
Homicide	2%
Trip	22%
Suicide gesture	70%
Suicide attempt	2%

were frequently just one more manifestation of long-standing problems. A diagnosis of suicide attempt, meaning a high probability that the individual's actions will result in death, was made in only one patient (subsequently diagnosed as schizophrenic). The diagnostic value of the structured interview is summarized in Table 1-10.

In one of the 50 cases, after the interview the diagnosis was changed to homicide. A 6-year-old boy and his mother had both ingested liquid lye, reportedly thinking it cider. The boy's statement that "Mommy said to drink it—we would live on a cloud in heaven and not have to see daddy anymore" led to the disclosure of an attempted homicide–suicide resulting from marital conflict.

The estimated lethality of intent was plotted against the total score for perturbation, the sum of all nine categories in the psychological biopsy as shown in Figure 1-4. Adolescents classified as intoxications had total scores ranging from 11 to 31, reflecting the frequency of overtly hostile behavior, prior self-destructive behavior, and stress in the form of family conflict. The total scores for the adolescents diagnosed as suicide gestures with minimal lethality of intent (0 to 2) were all below 30.

The seven patients considered to have made gestures of moderate lethality of intent all had total scores of 30 or above, as did the one subject considered to have made a true suicide attempt. This subject, diagnosed as schizophrenic, illustrates that the questionnaire defines social disruption but is of little value in rating the psychotic subject.

Although the "biopsy" outline used in this study does not clearly define the psychotic subject who may have a high suicide potentiality in the absence of apparent stress or perturbation, it does focus on factors that leave the subject with so few options that the threat of taking his own life in the only apparent way to solve his problems. It is also recognized that the high intercorrelations for stress, parental reactions, and extremes of parental control/expectation weigh the total score as possibly a better index of familial conflict than that of suicidal potentiality.

Scoring in all nine areas of perturbation was significantly higher for the subjects than for matched controls. The estimated lethality of intent had the highest correlation with the scores for depression, hostility, and stress. Hostility was scored higher than depression in 62 percent of the subjects but in only 36 percent of the controls. This is

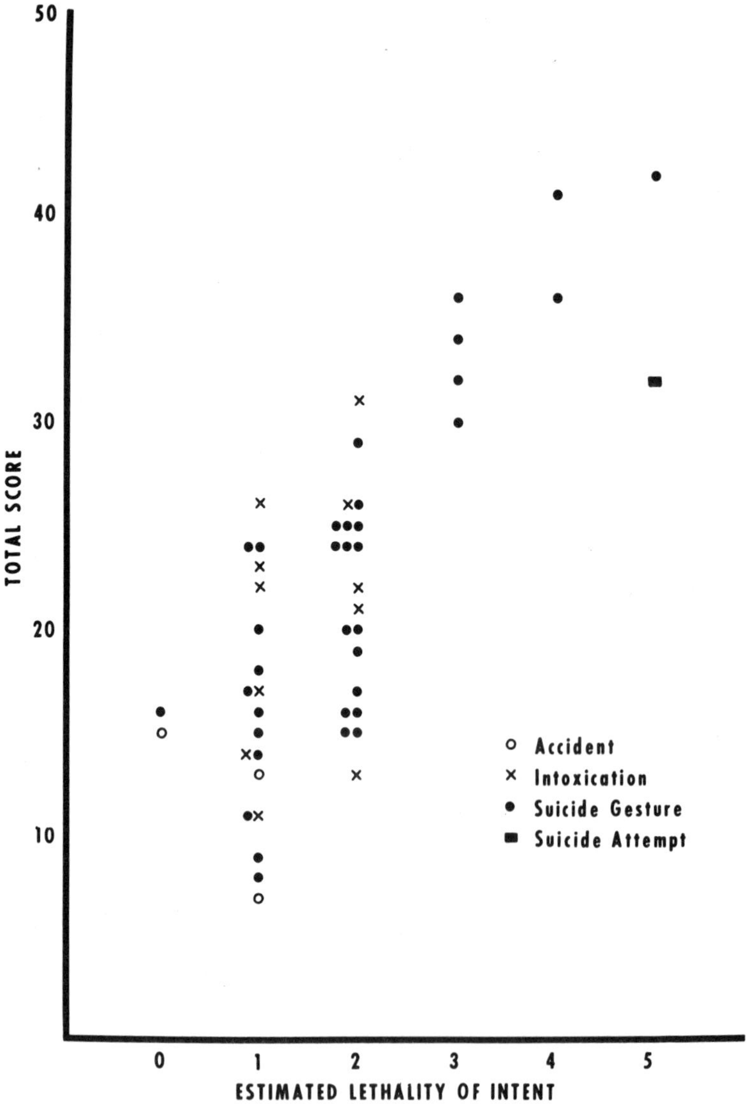

Fig. 1-4. Suicide Attempts in Children and Youth
The lethality of intent, rated from zero (none) to 10 (high) for 50 successive adolescents receiving emergency room treatment for poisoning. Lethality of intent was rated as minimal (0–2) for all those diagnosed as intoxications and for the majority of suicide gestures. *(Am J Dis Child 126:42–46, 1973. Copyright 1973, American Medical Association.)*

evidence, again, that depression of the suicide gesture is that of suppressed rage.

Loss of communication in the subjects related to both the extent and the chronicity of the difficulty. Fifty-six percent of the subjects and 48 percent of the controls could not communicate with one or both parents, but the controls retained a more open exchange with peers and other adults.

Parental reaction was seen as negative by most adolescents. Both subjects and controls had encountered stress in the form of divorce, stepparents, and economic deprivation; however, hostility, indifference, and overt rejection by the parent or parent-surrogate appeared to be the rule for the subjects and the exception for the controls. As shown in Table 1-11, 60 percent of the subjects, but only 14 percent

Table 1-11. Extremes and Divergence in Parental Attitudes

Control	*Expectations*	*Subjects (%)*	*Controls (%)*
Low	Low	28	10
	High	8	2
High or inconsistent	Low	14	2
	High	10	0
Total rated as extremely high or low in control/expectations		60	14

of the controls, reported a sense of extremes of parental control and expectations.

The extremes of parental control and expectations encountered in the subjects emerged as a dominant theme. On additional interviews and in subsequent counseling it became clear that these were salient characteristics in the subject's "psychological biopsy," and that peer conflicts and school difficulties were secondary phenomena.

Extreme parental control in the subjects was associated with high depression scores, usually equated with repressed hostility. When pervasive control is coupled with rejection in the form of negative or impossibly high expectations, the message to the child or abolescent becomes: "You are incapable," or "You are no good." This leads to the progressive loss of self-esteem recognized as a critical factor in the pathogenesis of depression. This repressed hostility and low self-esteem are commonly expressed as a suicide gesture or even a true suicide attempt.

In contrast to pervasive control and excessively high or negative expectations, a more frequent pattern emerged—that of parental rejection expressed as indifference. This pattern of low or inconsistent parental control combined with low expectations was associated with acting-out behavior manifested by intoxications and gestures of low lethality, and with hostility scores exceeding those of depression.

Extremes of parental reaction were seen most commonly in association with parental alcoholism, suggesting that these two related forms of self-destructive behavior, suicide and alcoholism, may be manifest as a self-perpetuating continuum in the parent and child.

These extremes of parental rejection suggest an obvious opportunity for benefit by placing the adolescent in a more favorable environment. The majority of these families are incapable of responding to psychotherapy; and to attempt therapy in these situations is futile.

The observation that 26 percent of patients already had a history of prior self-destructive behavior, and 32 percent had previous referral to a mental health agency, is analogous to the revolving-door therapy of the alcoholic. The delusion of the effectiveness of "referral for psychotherapy" is a manifestation of a faulty concept of the dynamics of self-destructive behavior in children and youth. Not only did these subjects have a high incidence of unsuccessful treatment, but they themselves predicted therapeutic failure: 10 of the 50 patients said they would probably die by suicide at some time. Because of the known and predicted recidivism in these adolescents, an investigation of the critical factors in recidivism seemed essential to define the total spectrum of self-destructive behavior.[9]

Self-destructive behavior in children and adolescents is a continuum ranging from recreational ingestions and intoxications to manipulative gestures (the equivalent of a suicide gesture) to self-destructive behavior of lethal intent. The socially acceptable diagnosis of accidental poisoning channels many adolescents with suicidal behavior to poison control centers. Extrapolating from national data, we estimate that each year poison control centers see over 250,000 intentional self-poisonings in children and youth alone. Along with poison control centers, primary care and emergency room physicians are the "gate-keepers" of suicide prevention. Training emergency room and poison control center personnel in a systematic evaluation of lethality of intent and perturbation provides an expedient means of dealing with this difficult problem.

REFERENCES

1. **Kessel N:** Self-poisoning. Br Med J 1: 1265–1270; 1336–1348, 1965
2. **McIntire M S, Angle C R:** The taxonomy of suicide as seen in poison control centers. Pediatri Clin North Am 17: 697–706, 1970
3. **McIntire M S, Angle C R:** Suicide as seen in poison control centers. Pediatrics 48: 914–922, 1971
4. **McIntire M S, Angle C R:** Is the poisoning accidental? Clin Pediatr 10: 414, 1971
5. **McIntire M S, Angle C R:** The psychological biopsy in self-poisoning of children and adolescents. Am J Dis Child 126: 42–46, 1973
6. **McIntire M S, Angle C R:** Evaluation of suicidal risk in adolescents. J Fam Pract 2: 339–341, 1975
7. **McIntire M S, Angle C R, Schlicht M L:** Suicide and self-poisoning in pediatrics. Adv Pediatr 24: 291–310, 1977
8. **McIntire M S, Angle C R, Struempler L J:** The concept of death in midwestern children and youth. Am J Dis Child 123: 527–532, 1972
9. **McIntire M S, Angle C R, Wikoff R L, Schlicht M L:** Recurrent adolescent behavior. Pediatrics 60: 605–608, 1977
10. **Monthly Vital Statistics Report:** Final Mortality Statistics, Vol 28, 1977. Washington DC, National Center for Health Statistics, Department of Health, Education and Welfare, Public Health Service, May 11, 1979
11. **Poison Control Statistics,** 1976, National Clearinghouse for Poison Control Centers, Food and Drug Administration; 5401 Westbard Avenue, Bethesda, Maryland 20016, Spring, 1978
12. **Shneidman E S:** Orientations toward death. In White R W: The Study Of Lives. New York, Atherton Press, 1966
13. **Shneidman E S:** Orientation toward cessation: a reexamination of current modes of death. J Forensic Sci 13: 33–45, 1968
14. **Vital Statistics of the United States,** Vol II, pp 1–248, 1–249, 7–150, 7–151. Washington DC, US Department of Health, Education and Welfare, Public Health Service 1975

two

recurrent adolescent suicidal behavior

Carol R. Angle

In our studies of the taxonomy of self-destructive behavior as seen in poison control centers, one of the most impressive elements was the frequency of prior events. In three successive studies, we found that from 26 percent to 52 percent of those studied had made one or more prior suicidal gestures, with almost all involving self-poisoning.[1-4, 7]

Since most self-destructive behavior by adolescents is of low lethality, an attempt was made to arrive at more significant predictors of repeated self-destructive behavior. The goal was to distinguish those at risk for repeated self-destructive behavior of low lethality from those at risk for gestures of increasing lethality of intent.

DETERMINING AND HANDLING SELF-DESTRUCTIVE BEHAVIOR

To investigate this, a group of 50 adolescents (40 females and 10 males), aged 14 to 18, who were successively admitted to three psychiatric services in Omaha following self-destructive behavior, were evaluated by the psychological biopsy.[5, 6, 8] The group had moved frequently but we were able to obtain a follow-up 6 to 24 months after the initial interview in 26 subjects (2 at 6 months, 13 at 1 year, and 11 at 24 months).

The structured interview outlined in Table 1-7 was conducted by a paraprofessional with special training in suicidology. The validity of this assessment was established by the concordance of ratings as given by the suicidologist and a psychiatrist. As outlined in Table 8 of Chapter 1, each subject was rated on a scale of 0–9 for:

1. Circumstantial lethality—the probability of rescue
2. Prior self-destructive behavior
3. Depression or negative self-concept
4. Hostility
5. Stress
6. Reaction of parent or parent surrogate
7. Loss of communication
8. Lack of supportive resources
9. Extremes of parental expectations and control

Based on the interview and the circumstances of the original event, each subject was then categorized according to:

1. **Lethality of intent**—low, medium, or high (based on probability of rescue)
2. **Diagnostic category**—intoxication, manipulative gesture, depressive gesture, true attempt
3. **Functional and social incapacitation**—none, mild, moderate, high
4. **Estimated risk** for repeated suicidal behavior.

Risk was rated high if lethality of intent was medium or high or if a gesture of low intent was coupled with prior suicidal behavior, significant depression, or thought disturbance.

The 26 adolescents available for follow-up evaluation were representative of the original 50 subjects. None of the original or follow-up subjects were depicted as having a high lethality of intent. Social incapacitation (defined as moderate to severe difficulties in functioning) was noted in 62 percent of the original group and 70 percent of those reevaluated. Of the original 50, 52 percent had made prior gestures, compared to 50 percent of the follow-up subjects. Of the original group, 44 percent had an alcoholic parent, similar to the 50 percent incidence for the follow-up group. Thought disturbances were present in 10 percent of the original and 15 percent of the follow-up group.

Of the follow-up group of 26 subjects, risk had been predicted as low for 6 subjects and high for 20 subjects by both the suicidologist and the psychiatrist (Table 2-1). The six "low-risk" subjects had all made gestures of negligible lethality of intent—predominantly drug and alcohol overdoses. They had a high incidence of social incapacitation with antisocial, delinquent behavior and high ratings for hostility. Only one had made a prior gesture, none were significantly depressed, and none had disturbed thinking.

Table 2-1. Predicted Risk for Recidivism in 26 Adolescents

	No. (%) of Subjects With Predicted Risk	
	Low	*High*
Number of subjects	6	20
Lethality of intent		
Minimal	6 (100)	–
Low—moderate	–	20 (100)
Depression/negative self concept rating>median	0	13 (65)
Hostility rating>median	5 (87)	6 (30)
Prior gestures	1 (15)	12 (60)
Thought disturbance	0	4 (20)
Alcoholic parent	2 (33)	11 (55)
Social incapacitation	4 (67)	14 (70)

A prediction of high risk of recurrent self-destructive behavior correlated best with the lethality of intent or probability of rescue in the original event, with prior suicidal gestures and with high ratings for depression or depression–hostility. The presence of moderate to severe functional incapacitation was unrelated to the prediction. Prior suicidal gestures had been made by 60 percent of the predicted high risk group and disturbed thought was diagnosed in 20 percent.

RECURRENCE

As outlined in Table 2-2 the overall recurrence rate was 31 percent, with 8 repeated attempts in 26 subjects. There was, however, a distinct difference between those predicted as low risk and those considered at high risk.

Table 2-2. Outcome at 6–24 Months

	Low Risk	*High Risk*	*Total*
Number of subjects	6	20	26
Suicidal behavior	0 (0)	8 (40)	8 (31)
Other problems	4 (66)	15 (75)	19 (73)
Institution	1 (15)	5 (25)	6 (23)
Improved	3 (50)	3 (15)	6 (23)

The 6 subjects considered at low risk had no recurrences. Prediction of risk was 100 percent reliable in the low-risk subjects of this study. They were identified by the low lethality of intent, past history of acting-out and delinquent behavior, and relatively high ratings for both hostility and self-esteem. The low-risk group continued to have significant problems (particularly alcoholism and conflict with the law) but half of the low-risk group improved.

Of the 20 high-risk subjects, 40 percent made repeated gestures—five within six months, two more by one year, and one by the second year. Only three were improved. Acting-out, delinquent behavior, and alcoholism persisted in three subjects. Three continued to have incapacitating thought disturbances. The dominant response in the other 11 was one of depression and entrapment related to poverty, alcoholic parents, chronic illness (two subjects), unwanted pregnancy (two subjects), homosexual guilt (one subject), and a life-long inability to cope with a multitude of problems.

Recidivism was primarily related to the subjects' failure to change their circumstances or the inability to respond to environmental change. In the 6 subjects moving to an improved environment, 2 in their own home and 4 in foster homes, there were no repeated gestures. The move itself appeared fortuitous since 2 of 6 foster homes were unsuccessful. In these 2 cases, unsuccessful foster home placement led to sequential foster homes and institutions; 1 of these subjects made a repeated gesture while at an interval youth center (Table 2-3).

Table 2-3. Therapy and Recidivism

	Total No.	*No. (%) of Subjects Making Gestures*
Total	26	8 (31)
Environment		
Worse	9	5 (56)
Better	6	0
Foster home	6	1 (15)
Recurrent institutionalization	6	5 (88)
Therapy>2 months	9	5 (56)
Thought disturbance	4	1 (25)

Institutionalization for 9 subjects was even less successful. Three of these were at reform school or prison, one was still incarcerated at the time of follow-up, but one had made a good adjustment at home. Of the 6 subjects who required prolonged psychiatric institutionalization, 5 were still hospitalized at the time of follow-up and 5 had made repeated suicide gestures.

Any predictive correlation of the duration of therapy with repetitive gestures is obscured by the fact that subjects with extreme perturbation in multiple spheres required prolonged therapy. All 26 subjects were initially dismissed at 2 to 6 weeks. Therapy for over eight weeks was received by 9 subjects, all with severe functional disability, including 3 with thought disturbances. None of the 9 with prolonged therapy were considered improved.

Subjects with a thought disturbance had a poor overall prognosis. Of the four subjects with a thought disturbance, three went from one institution to another and one of these made a repeated suicide gesture; one deteriorated after being sent home but then made a surprisingly good adjustment with foster parents.

Overall, the recurrence rate was 31 percent and the relative risk ratio was highest for the severely depressed, those with thought disturbances, and those with a deteriorating environment:

	Risk Ratio
Total	1.0
Thought disturbance	2.4
Depression above 75th percentile	2.8
Environment worse	2.4
Need for continued therapy	1.6

Psychiatric hospitalization with a return to an unchanged environment was uniformly unsuccessful. In many of these cases, the degree of incapacitation became more manifest. It was also reinforced by repeated institutionalization and failure to improve.

RESOURCES

The present methods of management, psychotherapy, and parental counseling are appalling. In all of our studies, the majority of the families were already known to social agencies, but the suicide gesture pointed out the crucial need for intervention. Frequently, the family situations were beyond repair. In these cases, we found the best results in adolescents who were able to move to a more favorable home situation with a relative or friend. These adolescents, however, are the product of years of familial and socioeconomic stress, and are often unattractive, rebellious, sullen or withdrawn. Therefore, foster home acceptance is unlikely for the older and more intractable adolescent.

In the changing shift in problems confronting children and youth, the child health professional must take the initiative for earlier intervention in the unremitting cycle of self-destructive behavior. Recommended are parenthood courses for both the high school student and the young parent. Problem families should be referred at the earliest possible moment. Foster home placement of preadolescents may be in the best interests of the child. Therapeutic programs should be implemented early to help the young child handle the dynamics of interpersonal conflict and to learn the coping mechanisms of social interactions.

THE ROLE OF THE HEALTH PROFESSIONAL

The magnitude of self-destructive behavior in young children becomes apparent when analyzing data from poison control centers. This enters the domain of public health and is the earliest manifestation of three major problems: alcoholism, drug abuse, and suicide. These are complex and interrelated manifestations that require new methods of analysis including education and socioeconomics.

Just as the health professions provided the leadership for early detection and development of needed programs for the retarded during the 1960s, they should respond as well now to the new challenge of childhood decompensation in the disturbed family environment.

REFERENCES

1. **McIntire MS, Angle CR:** The taxonomy of suicide as seen in poison control centers. Pediatr Clin North Am 17: 697–706, 1970
2. **McIntire MS, Angle CR:** Is the poisoning accidental? Clin Pediatr 10: 414, 1971
3. **McIntire MS, Angle CR:** Suicide as seen in poison control centers. Pediatrics 48: 914–922, 1971
4. **McIntire MS, Angle CR:** The psychological biopsy in self-poisoning of children and adolescents. Am J Dis Child 126: 42–46, 1973
5. **McIntire MS, Angle CR:** Evaluation of suicidal risk in adolescents. J Fam Pract 2: 339–341, 1975
6. **McIntire MS, Angle CR, Schlicht ML:** Suicide and self-poisoning in pediatrics. Adv Pediatr 24: 291–310, 1977
7. **McIntire MS, Angle CR, Struempler LJ:** The concept of death in midwestern children and youth. Am J Dis Child 123: 527–532, 1972
8. **McIntire MS, Angle CR, Wikoff RL, Schlicht ML:** Recurrent adolescent behavior. Pediatrics 60: 605–608, 1977

three

evaluating the suicidal adolescent

John Y. Donaldson and
James A. Davis

When a physician evaluates an adolescent who has made a suicide threat or an actual attempt, it is with several goals in mind. These include diagnosing any underlying psychiatric conditions, determining the need for further care, and preventing any future suicidal act. Such an evaluation requires that the clinician simultaneously bring together a number of skills. Ideally, the interviewer would first establish rapport with the patient and his family. The very act of establishing a positive relationship helps in beginning the therapeutic process. This same positive relationship helps the clinician to obtain needed information about the patient. After data has been collected concerning past history, current life situation, and present mental status, the degree of lethal intent and the most appropriate type of intervention most likely required can be established. In many respects, the fact that the patient is in crisis will greatly increase the impact of the physician's efforts.[14]

ESTABLISHING RAPPORT

In some medical specialties it is possible and occasionally desirable to maintain an aloof and rather authoritarian doctor–patient relationship. When dealing with a suicidal adolescent, you are very likely to be working with a person who has lost most of his or her capacity to see adult authority figures as positive resources. If the physician can establish a bond of trust with the patient, the patient's belief in being helped will increase and the risk of suicide will begin to diminish. The difficulty in establishing rapport can provide important information regarding the degree of the patient's alienation and sense of isolation.

In general, good rapport is best established by using certain interview techniques. One especially useful technique for relating to adolescents is client-centered therapy, a technique developed by Carl Rogers.[13] Its main features include genuineness, unconditional positive regard, and a reflective technique of interpretation also known as accurate empathy. Here, the interviewer would ideally be sympathetic and sensitive to the patient's most immediate mental state, acknowledging his or her anger, sorrow, or panic, while indicating his desire to help with the patient's problem. In addition, concepts from transactional analysis may also be helpful if one wants to avoid having the doctor–patient interaction deteriorate into the more negative aspects of the parent–child paradigm.[2] It is acceptable to function in a parental role if the patient seems to be in need of nonpossessive nurturance. However, one should avoid assuming a parental role as it involves an authoritarian, critical, or controlling type of interaction, particularly during the period of information-gathering. These same techniques are often helpful in gaining additional information from the patient's parents, who will very often have relationship problems themselves, ranging from controlling and critical, to hysterical and defensive, to aloof and preoccupied with their own life problems. Your assessment of the parents' typical mode of interaction and ability to help the patient will be as important in your understanding of the case as your assessment of the patient.

The overall goal is to create an atmosphere of concern and willingness to help without criticizing the patient. This approach can be as important in helping to discover unannounced suicidal intent as in assessing the risks of future acts once an actual attempt or threat has occurred. These techniques do have the disadvantage of being somewhat more time-consuming and emotionally draining for the clinician.

More detailed information about these evaluation techniques can be obtained by reading *Client Centered Therapy* by Carl Rogers and *Games People Play* by Eric Berne.[2, 13] One especially good synthesis of Rogerian techniques and transactional analysis can be found in the book, *Parent Effectiveness Training*, by Thomas Gordon.[9]

GATHERING AND ORGANIZING INFORMATION

By the time a relationship has begun to develop, you will have gathered a considerable amount of information about the patient. The most effective way to obtain and organize the needed information is by the standard psychiatric evaluation. This typically includes the chief complaint, history of present illness, social and developmental history, medical history, and mental status examination. The history of present illness may include the patient's past psychiatric history as well as a personal account of the events leading up to the suicide attempt. The social and developmental history section should be included whenever possible and may be obtained from family or friends. This should include confirming information regarding the patient's current life situation as well as providing information about significant past relationships, life stresses, personal losses, or the lack of significant relationships. This portion should also include information regarding the patient's style of relating and problem solving (*i.e.*, does the patient internalize or act out) and whether or not the patient is dependable. A brief medical history is included to ascertain the degree of health concern. The mental status examination is a standardized method of recording the patient's current emotional condition. A typical mental status examination includes the following sections: general appearance, behavior and attitude, his stream of mental activity (can the patient reach goal ideas?), content and trends of thought (is the patient delusional?), affect and mood, sensorium and mental capacity (is the patient organically impaired?), and insight and judgment. With such information, it is usually possible to either make a diagnosis or establish a differential diagnosis.

CONSIDERATION OF DIAGNOSIS

The most serious categories of mental illness are the functional psychoses, which are defined as those conditions in which the patient has lost contact with reality without a physical (organic) explanation. In adolescence, schizophrenia and manic-depressive illness are the most frequently seen psychoses. In the former, the "4 A's" of autism, ambivalence, loose associations, and inappropriate affect are present.[3] Manic-depressive illness is a more difficult diagnosis to establish in the adolescent. In the manic type, flight of ideas, hostility, and grandiose thinking are present, while in the depressed type one sees decreased psychomotor activity, excessive sleeping, and occasional catatonic posturing.

Patients with a neurosis are troubled by increased anxiety that is out of proportion to their situation. The source of the anxiety may be constitutional, but more typically it is secondary to unconscious conflict and repressed emotions. The neurotic subtypes are determined by their most characteristic defense mechanism. The hysterical neurotic in adolescence usually presents with dissociative and conversion symptoms. They are relatively unlikely to suicide because their symptoms tend to relieve them from responsibility. In the depressive neurosis, some form of object loss has often occurred and the patient may suicide because of his or her reaction to the loss. The obsessive-compulsive neurotic may attempt suicide because of overwhelming anxiety about his condition. This patient's behavior is "ego alien" and the patient often acts in desperation because he or she feels this obsession or compulsion cannot be controlled. In the phobic patient, suicidal behavior may ensue because of panic after the patient is confronted by the phobic situation.

A third major category includes the psychophysiologic illness. In this pattern, the patient converts anxiety into a physical symptom in an organ innervated by the autonomic nervous system. The most typical examples involve the gastrointestinal system. In adolescence, psychophysiologic disorders affecting the skin and the respiratory and genitourinary systems are also common.

Organic brain syndromes are those conditions in which there is physical brain impairment affecting judgment, orientation, memory, affect, and cognition. Examples of this category would be cerebral tumor, a seizure disorder, electrolyte imbalance, thyroid disease, or a drug induced psychosis. There are six major categories of chemical dependency: narcotic dependency, minor tranquilizer, sedative–hypnotic, stimulant, hallucinogen and cannabis, and alcohol abuse. Frequent abuse of any of these substances is associated with an increased incidence of suicidal behavior.

Personality disorders are patterns of behavior in which the person has a limited capacity for psychologically honest and intimate relationships combined with a tendency toward a variety of self-defeating acts. There is a tendency to avoid making this diagnosis in early adolescence unless the pattern is striking.

The antisocial person is impulsive, hedonistic, and glib, and lives by the pleasure principle, and his or her wits (90% are male). He lacks a superego so nothing is forbidden. The sociopath "wants what he wants when he wants it and he wants it now." The hysterical personality is usually a woman who is seductive, flirtatious, coquettish, and unbelievably naive. She is often manipulated by men, especially antisocial men, but she is just as likely to relate in a manipulative fashion herself. In the paranoid personality, one sees no sense of humor, extreme jealousy, overutilization of the ego defense projection, and all or no anger. This type of person is more likely to attack someone than to suicide. In the obsessive-compulsive personality, one sees conformity, rigidity, a need to control, and an extremely idealistic self-image which sets the person up for disappointment. The schizoid is shy, introverted, and withdrawn, and experiences much psychic pain in adolescence because of poor peer interaction. The cyclothymic personality is characterized by mood swings which are unexplained by life events and can lead to suicidal behavior at anytime in adolescence. In the passive-aggressive personality, one sees the "clinging vine," the bully, and the two-faced gossip. These disorders are the most prevalent of any psychiatric condition and, unfortunately, the patient usually has little insight into his behavior because of a tendency to rationalize and deny reality. If one is to diagnose all adolescents with suicidal behavior, the majority will be in the personality disorder category.[5]

In the final group, involving sexual dysfunction, one sees some of the most dramatic suicides. In adolescence, there is a great need to succeed in establishing sexual role development. The patient who sees himself as failing at this task is frequently depressed and withdrawn. Patients who combine sexual orientation disturbances with personality disorders seem to be especially at risk.

Case History 1

Current Complaints. Recent suicide gestures

History of Present Illness. This 17-year-old adolescent male presented himself for outpatient therapy over ten years ago at the request of his mother following a recent overdose with a proprietary medication. At the time of the intake, the patient described himself as an active homosexual who had just spent what he described as three of the happiest months of his life being kept in a plush penthouse apartment by a prominent local interior decorator. Immediately prior to the suicide attempt, he had fallen out of favor with the decorator, had been asked to leave the apartment, and had been replaced by another young man. The patient was very conscious of grieving his loss and was able to describe both his sorrow and his anger. He was also very definite in stating that he did not want any type of therapy for his homosexual behavior.

Family History. The patient is the youngest of four children. His father died of complications of alcoholism when the patient was a preadolescent. For the past few years, he has been the only child at home with his mother. The patient and his mother are not particularly close. The patient has dropped out of school, does not work steadily, and has few friends.

Medical History. Noncontributory

Mental Status Examination

GENERAL APPEARANCE, BEHAVIOR, AND ATTITUDE. This patient is striking in that he is 6 feet 5 inches tall, but obviously effeminate. He lacks physiologic signs of anxiety.

STREAM OF MENTAL ACTIVITY. The patient is verbal and reaches goal ideas without difficulty. No looseness of association is noted.

AFFECT AND MOOD. The patient's affect is somewhat dramatic. His mood is fairly consistently depressed, but he is capable of momentarily brightening as seemed appropriate for the content of the conversation.

CONTENT OF THOUGHT. The patient shows no delusions. He is very obviously preoccupied with his recent loss, but not to the point of having obsessions.

SENSORIUM AND MENTAL CAPACITY. The patient's sensorium and mental capacity indicate good recent and remote memory and better than average intellectual ability.

INSIGHT AND JUDGMENT. Insight and judgment are good in the sense that the patient seems to understand the acute nature of his illness, but poor in that he has much less insight into the more pervasive aspects of his psychopathology. He has shown some history of impulsive behavior which suggests that at times his judgment may be poor.

IMPRESSION.
1. Adjustment reaction with depressed mood
2. Personality disorder with mixed passive-aggressive and hysterical features
3. Homosexuality (This was included in the then current nomenclature.)

SUMMARY. This young man responded rapidly but superficially to weekly psychotherapy over the course of several months. He failed numerous appointments and eventually dropped out of therapy. He hoped to become a hairdresser. He temporarily resumed his high school work through an individual study program, but later dropped out. He began to work, but quit after a few weeks. His original treatment actually occurred over ten years ago. For many years he was lost to follow-up. When he was 26 years of age, it was noted in a news article that he did successfully commit suicide with carbon monoxide. The details of his distress at that time are not available.

In the broad category of behavior disorders of childhood and adolescence, there is one condition that is somewhat more likely to contain suicide as a component. It is the hyperkinetic reaction which has yielded to a newer term, attention deficit disorder. As children, these patients have little ability to sit still or maintain concentration for even brief periods of time. When adolescence (puberty) arrives, the hyperactivity usually disappears, but not all of these children achieve a normal mental status. Many continue to be troubled by impulsive behavior and poor judgment. The remainder of these patients seem to develop increasing tendencies to be withdrawn, anxious, or delinquent. Typically, all of these patients will have reached the level of a personality disorder, psychosis, or neurosis by the time the suicidal gesture or act has occurred in late adolescence.[15]

The final group of behaviors, termed **transient situational disturbances** on the adjustment reactions, comprise the most common diagnostic category for adolescent psychiatric patients. There is a great tendency to use this diagnosis since it is simple, straightforward, and implies an excellent prognosis regardless of the treatment modality employed. Simply defined, a transient situational disturbance is a normal person's reaction to overwhelming stress, the most common symptoms of which are anxiety and depression or both. For this type of patient a suicide attempt may be the ultimate act of desperation or the ultimate plea for help.

ASSESSING INFORMATION TO PREDICT RISK

After gathering information about the patient, there will still be the need to consider the degree of immediate risk, which will in turn help in the choice of treatment. Because suicidal behavior or intent in adolescents may have a variety of causes and can be expressed in so many different ways, the assessment of risk is difficult. Unsuccessful suicide attempts may vary from the nearly fatal with obvious lethal intent, to a desperate, low-lethality plea for help, to very minor gestures with clearly manipulative intent. All attempts can be seen as a statement that something is very wrong in the adolescent's life which he or she feels powerless to change, either alone or with the help normally available.[7]

EVALUATING PATIENTS WITH EXPRESSED LETHAL INTENT

The patients with the most severe lethality can first be discovered by the seriousness of their injury or self-poisoning or by the nature of the acts they were narrowly prevented from carrying out. The risk of lethal intent increases as the severity of the patient's interpersonal discomfort increases compared to the quality of his or her life situation and the interpersonal resources available. These seriously disturbed patients may continue to express sincere dismay at being rescued and may continue to be withdrawn and show gross depression. (Degree of lethality has been discussed at some length in Chap. 1 and in other articles by Dr. McIntire and coworkers.[11,12])

One very common example of this type of patient is the young schizophrenic who has some insight into his illness, who remains extremely uncomfortable despite treatment and family support, and who sees no chance of significant improvement. A decision to terminate their existence is most commonly made by these patients when they are in their twenties or thirties, but may occasionally be made during late adolescence. The common denominator is a loss of hope.[1] In general, patients in this group express the belief that their condition is so painful and so chronic that they cannot face an indefinite period of continuing intense suffering.

Case History 2

Current Complaints. "I couldn't stand it any longer."

History of Present Illness. This 19-year-old woman recently overdosed with her psychotropic medication and was unconscious for 2 days following the attempt. When she was able to talk, she described her severe discomfort despite repeated efforts by several psychiatrists to regulate her medication. She spoke of a complete loss of hope of becoming well. Six months prior to this near-lethal attempt, she had precipitously broken off her first successful romantic involvement with a young man. She has been previously hospitalized five times since the age of 12 because of depression and psychosis.

Family History. The patient is the second of three children. There is a strong family history of psychiatric illness on the father's side. The father is said to be aloof and somewhat schizoid. The patient's mother is more energetic and outgoing, but reportedly quite critical of the patient. The older sister is said to be very domineering and had always spoken for the patient when she was younger.

Medical History. Negative for other illnesses

Mental Status Examination

GENERAL APPEARANCE, BEHAVIOR, AND ATTITUDE. The patient is a slightly obese young woman who is rather aloof and reluctant to reveal much information to her therapist. She is quite anxious.

STREAM OF MENTAL ACTIVITY. Her speech is often blocked by internal thoughts. At times she shows looseness of association. She is best able to reach goal ideas when she is angry.

AFFECT AND MOOD. Her affect tends to be quite flat. At times, she seems to smile inappropriately. Her most consistent mood is one of depression.

CONTENT OF THOUGHT. She is most obsessed with her disability. She compares herself negatively to her age mates who are more successful in school, beginning to start work, or having significant close relationships with the opposite sex.

SENSORIUM AND MENTAL CAPACITY. The patient complains of some recent memory loss, and her remote memory is not as good as one would expect. Her intellectual ability is better than average and she has a history of doing good school work when she is well compensated.

INSIGHT AND JUDGMENT. The patient is very painfully aware of the limitations imposed on her by her illness. She has at times shown impulsive behavior and is likely to remove herself from any type of unpleasant situation.

Impression. Chronic undifferentiated schizophrenia

Summary. This patient has been psychiatrically ill since the age of 12 and has had multiple psychiatric hospitalizations. She frequently shows signs of significant depression, paranoia, and thought disorder. At her best, she is aloof, distant, unpredictable, and mistrustful. She did respond slowly but positively to the addition of lithium to her psychotropic medications. Following several months in the hospital, she was released to an outpatient status and is being followed in long-term psychotherapy. She is being treated as a borderline patient at this point. Her desire to terminate her existence still surfaces from time to time and she continues to be seen as a significant suicide risk.

You may occasionally see similar behavior in medically ill patients; however, in conditions in which death is expected to be relatively swift (as in certain malignancies), the remaining months of life are more likely to be savored as an acceptable trade-off for future pain. As physical discomfort, probable disability, and projected life span increase (*i.e.*, chronic renal dialysis, patients with endogenous depression, or patients with other chronic disabling diseases), the risk of a suicidal act also increases.

A second group of patients with high lethality may be less uncomfortable physiologically but express more the idea of being unworthy to continue life. They may be schizophrenic and have a delusion of unworthiness, but more commonly they are seriously depressed. Simple acute grief will rarely cause a suicidal attempt; but grief which interfaces with guilt and anger may be a significant cause. This may involve the loss of a relationship for which the patient feels responsible; it may involve the loss of a relationship with a parent because of certain acts by the patient; it may involve the loss of some other significant person such as a love object; or may be due to loss of self-esteem. Adolescents who have lost their positive identity may also be at risk. Identity is the most important development task in this age group.[6]

Case History 3

Current Complaints. "I just couldn't stand it anymore!"

History of Present Illness. This 16-year-old sophomore at a parochial high school had been having problems with depression for most of the second semester of his sophomore year. Being quiet, shy, thin, and gangly, he was unable to find a comfortable position in either heterosexual or athletic roles. His primary interests included piano playing and he was seen by his classmates as being a "jerk." Academically he was a B+ student, but this placed him only in the upper third of his class, not high enough for the honor role which was an important achievement for his family. On the last day of spring vacation he made a suicide attempt with 100 500-mg acetamimophen tablets. After less than 10 minutes he announced the fact to his parents who took him to the closest emergency room. He was given an emetic and kept for observation to rule out potential liver damage.

Family History. The patient is the fifth of five children, all of whom are male and independent. Except for the patient, all the older siblings are either very successful students or are working and already have degrees. The father is a successful professional with rather obsessive–compulsive features in his personality. The mother is a relatively warm obsessive–compulsive.

Medical History. The patient is in good health, but has had multiple psychophysiologic complaints.

Mental Status Examination

GENERAL APPEARANCE, BEHAVIOR, AND ATTITUDE. This is a 16-year-old, thin, fair-complected youth who is alert, cooperative, and moderately anxious.

STREAM OF MENTAL ACTIVITY. Speech is spontaneous and productive.

AFFECT AND MOOD. Normal range of affect, moderately depressed mood

CONTENT AND TREND OF THOUGHT. No evidence of delusions. The patient is concerned about his health. He sees himself as a failure.

SENSORIUM AND MENTAL CAPACITY. The patient is oriented in all areas. His memory is very good and his intelligence is bright normal.

INSIGHT AND JUDGMENT. The patient appears to have unrealistic expectations for himself. He is over-controlled and unimpulsive.

IMPRESSION. 1. Depressive neurosis
2. Compulsive personality

SUMMARY. This 16-year-old adolescent was failing by his own

standards in all possible roles—academic, peer group, heterosexual, and athletic. This resulted in a critical disintegration of his self-concept and he saw suicide as the only solution. Short-term inpatient treatment in a medical facility and outpatient psychotherapy were successful in boosting his self-esteem. He appears to have a good prognosis.

In severe depressions, the most psychodynamic typical pattern involves a real or imagined loss of another person or a concept of self about which feelings are intense but ambivalent. In these situations, the negative aspects are nearly always as great as or greater than the positive aspects being mourned. Ambivalently held but significant relationships or concepts of self often involve a degree of repressed anger. In this situation, the loss of the positive aspect of the object is consciously experienced, but the anger about the negative factors is denied and may be turned against the self. When such a person becomes suicidal, he may choose an extremely violent means.

The underlying psychodynamics of psychotic and severely neurotic patients may overlap to a large extent. This is the type of patient that Freud described when he wrote of suicide as inverted murder (*i.e.*, extreme anger which cannot be expressed because that person is also a love object).[8] Other common psychodynamic causes as described by Herbert Hendin include death as a retaliatory abandonment, reunion, rebirth, self-punishment, and confirmation of feeling already dead.[10] Suicide can also be added as a statement of identification with a parent or other significant person who had already elected suicide.

An intermediate level of lethality involves a patient who may see himself in a hopeless environmental situation, often because of a series of losses, failures, unhappy relationships with the people he normally depends on. This type of patient often exhibits less intrinsic psychopathology than the group of patients with more clear-cut lethal intent. Their suicidal act is more often a genuine plea for outside help, or a way of clearly identifying to all concerned the seriousness of their situation. These patients come from the diagnostic category of acute situational or adjustment reactions. In most cases, their attempts are not truly manipulative, but instead are seen by the patient as the only way of dealing with a very difficult problem. Their lack of success at suicide often indicates their ambivalence about death.

Because these patients do not have a severe degree of psychopathology, it is very common for them to have a history of significant and satisfactory relationships. For this reason, it is often easier to establish rapport with patients in this group than with those in the earlier groups. In nearly all respects, these patients appear to have the best prognosis when proper intervention is undertaken.

Patients whose suicidal verbalizations or actions are clearly manipulative present a special problem for the clinician.[4] These are the most common and the least likely to be truly lethal. To ignore or belittle them increases the risk of escalating the seriousness of the attempt. However, the clinician must also be on guard to prevent the patient from enjoying significant secondary gains from such acts. Often such patients have a history of other forms of manipulative behavior such as hysterical outbursts, lying, stealing, drug abuse, or similar problems common in personality disorders. The suicide gesture in this case may be part of an effort to gain sympathy, attract attention, restore a failing relationship, or escape the consequences of some other action.

Case History 4

Current Complaints. I was angry at my mother.

History of Present Illness. The patient is a 15-year-old girl who was admitted at 2:00 a.m. by a first-year psychiatric house officer from the university hospital emergency room. The patient had earlier taken approximately 14 aspirin tablets after an argument with her mother. She had been denied an opportunity to go out with friends on a school night. The patient has had a marked exacerbation in her behavioral problems in the past two to three years which her mother feels was possibly due to the mother's second divorce and remarriage.

Family and Social History. The patient is the older of two siblings. Her parents were divorced when she was relatively young. Her mother was then married for several years to a man who was both charming and abusive. The patient was apparently significantly attached to him. For a time following the disintegration of this marriage, the patient lived with her maternal grandmother, and for the past two years since her mother's remarriage, she has lived with her mother and stepfather. The stepfather's work causes him to move approximately once every year.

Medical History. Negative

Mental Status Examination

GENERAL APPEARANCE, BEHAVIOR, AND ATTITUDE. When the patient was seen the day following admission, she appeared to be comfortable and cooperative. She did not show physiologic signs of anxiety.

STREAM OF MENTAL ACTIVITY. Her speech is spontaneous and productive.

AFFECT AND MOOD. Her affect first appeared to be under control. After several days she showed evidence of a considerable lability in her affect. Her mood showed some signs of mild depression, but this was not a consistent finding.

CONTENT AND TRANSIENT THOUGHT. The patient was very much concerned with here-and-now issues and did not appear to have any delusions or preoccupations.

SENSORIUM AND MENTAL CAPACITY. The patient was well oriented. Her recent and remote memory were intact. Her intellectual ability appeared to be in the average range.

INSIGHT AND JUDGMENT. The patient showed a marked tendency to be impulsive. At one point, she appeared to show some potential for developing some self-observation skills, but for the most part she remained impulsive and used a number of projective defenses to blame others for her problems.

DIAGNOSTIC IMPRESSION. Unsocialized disturbance of conduct

SUMMARY. This patient was admitted for a short period of time to rule out the possibility of a treatable depression. After working with her for several days, it became increasingly clear that she suffered from emotional detachment. She was in need of a structured environment, but not in need of psychiatric care as such. At the time of her discharge, she stole a hair dryer and some other items from the ward, which her mother later returned. Since her discharge we have had one inquiry from the juvenile court in this area and a later similar request for information from another state.

While it is tempting to discount these acts as annoying and not serious, they indicate serious problems in the patient's relationships to others as well as problems in the patient's coping skills. Many patients of this type will never make a serious suicidal attempt or progress to clearly lethal intent. Nevertheless, as a group they make up a significant number of successful suicides. Some of these patients become trapped because of a need to establish their credibility and therefore may feel compelled to make a lethal or very damaging gesture. Another subgroup may at some time, reach a point of such desperation that they will make a decision to commit suicide that has the same type of lethal intent as may be seen in seriously depressed patients who have lost hope. Typically, this is part of a reaction to their many failures in life which are secondary to their pattern of short-sighted and manipulative behavior.

EVALUATING RISK IN POTENTIALLY SUICIDAL PATIENTS

Signs of suicidal potential in patients who have not openly expressed suicidal intent are varied. One common situation which, unfortunately, is most often noted in retrospect involves the patient who comes to the doctor complaining of some vague physical discomfort and is found dead by his own hand several days later. This type of patient is often looking for an explanation for or relief of severe physiologic discomfort. One reason these patients are often missed is because so many patients present with complaints that have no physical basis. Patients who repeatedly present with a variety of physical complaints that are clearly without organic basis should be questioned about their sense of hopelessness regarding their condition and, ideally, given appropriate reassurance in a supportive and sympathetic manner. The best indication of a need to take a patient more seriously is when either a new patient presents with intense subjective distress or an established patient has begun to show a tendency to return for frequent reassessment of clearly psychophysiologic conditions.[14] A prime example would be the compulsive older adolescent, in despair over his or her first scholastic failure or serious social failure, and, at the same time, under pressure from one or both parents who are highly invested in the child's success. (Re-read Case History 3, but imagine the patient coming to your office two weeks earlier.) Such a patient will likely bottle-up his or her feelings, only to suffer both depression and somatic distress. One thing such patients tend to share is the tendency to be highly anxious. This anxiety is most typically psychogenic and related to a conflict between what the patient desires and the real or imagined wishes of the domineering parent. Physiologic signs of this anxiety include cold and sweaty hands, mottled skin, hyperactive deep tendon reflexes, and mild hypertension. When this type of patient expresses intense discomfort, it is appropriate to ask if the discomfort has led to consideration of suicide.

Another type of patient at risk is the depressed adolescent who has been emotionally neglected. Such a patient most commonly comes from a lower socioeconomic group, but may also come from affluent families where the parents have focused so intensely on meeting their own needs that they have neglected the patient. Typically these patients are somewhat detached and sometimes defiant. Usually they are free of physiologic signs of anxiety. Their suicidal intent is often unconscious and their risk is more subtle. They are not intensively uncomfortable and they are not seeking immediate release. However, they may express a sense of emptiness in their lives or a feeling of being without purpose. Such patients may engage in a variety of sensation-seeking behaviors including reckless driving, promiscuous sexual behavior, or drug abuse. Repeated and flagrant acts of this type are a significant sign of this type of depression and should be considered a type of suicidal behavior.

A summary of the most significant risk factors which can usually be discovered during the initial evaluation include:

1. All attempts of marked lethality
2. A psychotic patient who has decided life is too painful to continue

3. Patients with intense physiologic discomfort
4. Patients who have established a pattern of drug abuse that shows a total disregard for their physical safety
5. Patients with a history of previous suicide attempts
6. Patients who strongly identify with a person who has successfully committed suicide
7. Patients who combine intense anger with their depression
8. Patients without a positive or potentially positive social support system
9. Patients who either verbally or nonverbally have indicated that they have made a definite plan to terminate their existence.

PLANNING INTERVENTION

Adolescents who have expressed a lethal intent either by developing a clear-cut plan or by already acting in such a manner should receive psychiatric care as soon as possible. This will almost always be done on an inpatient basis and will require an exploration of the physical, psychogenic, and social causes of the individual patient's distress. The need for inpatient intervention is further increased if psychosis is present or if the patient has a previous history of depression.

Another group which may require hospital admission consists of those patients who are experiencing significant distress within their families or other living situations. This is the group with a relatively good prognosis that was discussed above. Often a period of psychiatric hospitalization helps to establish the fact that a patient's discomfort is situational rather than endogenous. Efforts must then be made to assess whether the patient can return to the pathologic environment, if an outside source of support could be found, or, if efforts could be made to improve the quality of that environment. In many cases, it will be necessary to place these patients in foster care or a type of structured group situation. To return them quickly to an unchanged environment creates a significant risk of further crisis with further pleas for help.

The patients who are suffering from personality disorders who make manipulative suicide gestures are especially difficult to assess and treat. Many of these patients can be returned home without hospital admission or after a very brief stay.[4] When hospitalized, these patients tend to be quite disruptive to the more seriously ill patients on a psychiatric ward. Brief or intermediate psychiatric care seems to do very little to change the personality structure of these patients. If resources permit, relatively long-term hospital care (*i.e.*, one to two years' duration) can be helpful in selected cases when efforts are made to significantly restructure the patient's personality through intensive psychotherapy. These patients, although presenting a small risk for individual attempts, present a great risk as a group partly because of their large number and partly because of their unpredictability. We feel that it is important to discuss these risks with the parents and other significant people. The clinician must somehow find a middle ground that prevents these patients from escalating their manipulative attempts or using them excessively in other ways. At the same time, the clinician should avoid overlooking the previously manipulative patient who has become so distressed that he or she is ready to make a lethal attempt.

Anxious or depressed patients who have multiple psychophysiologic symptoms and who have considered suicide (but are not overtly suicidal) will often respond to brief office psychotherapy and efforts to help them understand their discomforts and relieve their distress. If a persistent anxiety continues or if a patient fails to find relief in his or her discussions with the primary physician, a psychiatric referral, usually on an outpatient basis, is indicated. Occasionally, such a patient will break down and reveal very clear lethal suicidal intent which will require more active intervention and hospitalization.

The depressed, detached adolescent who may not overtly express suicidal intent but whose behavior implies a lack of value for life will also likely benefit from psychiatric intervention. Some of these patients will have relatively untreatable personality disorders, but many appear to be caught in a vicious cycle of apathy, school failure, social failure, and drug abuse that can be interrupted through a significant psychotherapeutic relationship. These patients may need to be hospitalized when their thrill-seeking behavior or drug use escalates to life-threatening or sanity-threatening proportions.

SUMMARY

In evaluating the actively or potentially suicidal adolescent patient, it is important for the clinician to be aware that many causes, symptoms, and signs can be associated with this one broad class of deviant behavior. Intervention may vary from office psychotherapy by the primary physician, to outpatient intervention by a psychiatrist, to intensive inpatient psychiatric care. Because of the many different reasons for suicidal behavior, it is important to intervene in a way that is lifesaving but at the same time avoids providing the patient with undue secondary gain. Information to be used in making such a judgment can be best gained by first establishing rapport and then using certain interview techniques which both begin the therapeutic process and facilitate the gathering of information. The information gathered can then be used to determine the seriousness of intent and the level of risk. These same interview techniques can also be helpful in discovering patients who have not overtly expressed or acted out a suicidal intent.

REFERENCES

1. **Bech AT, Kovacs M, Weissman A et al:** Hopelessness and suicidal behavior: an overview JAMA 234 (11): 1146–1149, 1975
2. **Berne E:** Games People Play. New York, Grove Press, 1964
3. **Bleuher EP:** Dementia Praecox on the Group of Schizophrenia. New York, International Universities Press, 1950
4. **Cowen J:** The suicide threat—when is it for real? Resident and Staff Physician 20 (9): 65–72, 1974
5. **Crumley FE:** Adolescent suicide attempts. JAMA 241 (22): 2404–2407, 1979
6. **Erikson EH:** Eight ages of man. In Harrison S, McDermott J (eds): Childhood Psychopathology. New York, International Universities Press, 1972
7. **Fischer HK:** Faces and masks of depression: the psychodynamic side. Psychosomatics 20 (4): 254–268, 1979
8. **Freud S:** Mourning and melancholia. In Collected Papers, pp 152–170. London, Hogarth Press, 1940
9. **Gordon T:** Parent Effectiveness Training. New York, PH Wyden, 1970
10. **Hendin H:** Psychiatric emergencies. In Friedman AM, Kaplan HS (eds): Comprehensive Textbook of Psychiatry. Baltimore, Williams & Wilkins, 1967
11. **McIntire MS, Angle CR:** Evaluation of suicide risk in adolescents. Fam Prac 2 (5): 339–341, 1975

12. **McIntire MS, Angle CR, Wikoff RL, Schlicht ML:** Recurrent adolescent suicidal behavior. Pediatrics [Suppl] 60: 605–608, 1977
13. **Rogers CR:** Client-Centered Therapy. Boston, Houghton Mifflin, 1951
14. **Ruben HL:** Managing suicidal behavior. JAMA 241 (3): 282–284, 1979
15. **Weiss G, Hechtman L, Perlman T et al:** Hyperactives as young adults: a controlled prospective ten-year follow up of 75 children. Arch Gen Psychiatry 36: 675–681, 1979

four

diagnosis and treatment of acute overdose in adolescents

Frederick H. Lovejoy, Jr.

Optimal diagnosis and management of drug overdose in the adolescent requires considering the epidemiology of the involved drugs as well as clearly understanding their pharmacology.[3,5] The involved drugs fall into four classes: depressant drugs, excitatory drugs, narcotics, and hallucinogenic agents. Drugs falling within a given class have similar clinical effects and, based on similar pharmacologic properties, often involve a similar approach to therapy. Commonly used drugs in the depressant class include: barbiturates, benzodiazepines, alcohol, glutethamide, phenothiazines and inhaled hydrocarbons. Drugs in the stimulant class include amphetamines and cocaine. In the narcotic class, opium, heroin, methadone, propoxyphene and pentazocine are most often involved. The most commonly used hallucinogenic agents include phencyclidine (PCP) and, to a lesser extent, anticholinergic drugs.

EPIDEMIOLOGY

The frequency of use of these agents among adolescents will vary from month to month and from city to city throughout the United States. For those treating drug overdose in adolescents, it becomes most important to be familiar with those drugs in current use at any given time. An example is a listing of the most commonly used drugs in Boston in 1978, obtained from a survey of drug prevention services, crises centers, hotlines, ambulance services, neighborhood health centers, youth resource centers, the criminal justice system, and the poison information center.[19] These data, while not quantifiable in an absolute sense, do serve as a rough indicator of those overdoses the clinician might expect to encounter. These include: 1) alcohol; 2) phencyclidine; 3) heroin; 4) marihuana; 5) benzodiazepines; 6) cocaine; 7) propoxyphene; 8) amphetamines; 9) barbiturates; 10) hallucinogens.

Knowledge of the sex and age of the patient may also help in arriving at a diagnosis. For example, from the same survey in Boston, heroin, methadone, and cocaine are used more commonly by males while tranquilizers, amphetamines, and psychotherapeutic drugs are used more frequently by females. Among adolescents less than 14 years of age, inhaled drugs (volatile hydrocarbons) are the most abused. In the 14 to 17 age group, phencyclidine and amphetamines are most frequent, and in those 18 to 21 alcohol, phencyclidine and barbiturates presents the greatest problem. Finally, knowledge of the neighborhood of origin of the poisoned adolescent may also be helpful in identifying the drug of abuse. For example, alcohol, cocaine and phencyclidine predominate in the more affluent areas of Boston while opium, heroin and alcohol have greatest use in the lower socioeconomic areas.

HISTORY AND PHYSICAL EXAMINATION

A pertinent history should explore medical and non-medical use of psychoactive drugs as well as the frequency, amount, and duration of their use. In addition, the history should include previous episodes of overdose, suicide gesture, and suicide attempts. Finally, medical illnesses that may be worsened or may obscure a clinical diagnosis (i.e. seizure disorders, diabetes mellitus, hypertension and pulmonary disease) should also be elicited.

A careful physical examination will often assist in arriving at a diagnosis. The time of appearance of signs and symptoms will depend on the route of exposure, the dose, and the length of use of the drug. Agents inhaled or taken by the intravenous route will result in earlier signs and symptoms than those taken by the oral route. The severity of signs and symptoms will increase with increasing dose. Finally, increasing length of use will result in tolerance; the phenomenon of decreasing clinical effect and the need for increased dosage with prolonged use.

Hypertension, tachycardia, and hyperpyrexia are commonly seen with phencyclidine, amphetamines, and anticholinergic agents. Hypotension, bradycardia, and hypothermia are more frequent with depressant drugs and narcotic agents. Excitation, agitation, disordered sensorium, depression, ataxia, and seizures may all occur with abused drugs. Stimulant drugs commonly cause increased motor activity and an agitated state. Depressant drugs and narcotic agents cause excitation at low dose, while at a high dose, they cause central nervous system (CNS) depression. Stimulant drugs, short-acting barbiturates, narcotics, and anticholinergic drugs can cause convulsions.

Pupillary size is also helpful in establishing a diagnosis. The constricted pupil indicates a narcotic agent, though barbiturates, alcohol, phenothiazines and phencyclidine may also produce small pupils.[16] Alternatively, dilated pupils are seen with amphetamines, anticholinergic agents and drug withdrawal. Horizontal and vertical nystagmus are commonly seen with phencyclidine and horizontal nystagmus with barbiturates. Signs of increased sympathetic nervous system activity, sweating, dry mouth, nausea, vomiting, agitation and pilomotor response, are seen with drug withdrawal. Old scars and needle track marks indicate intravenous use of drugs. Finally, alcohol and volatile hydrocarbons emit a distinctive odor thereby facilitating their identification.

DIFFERENTIAL DIAGNOSIS

Other medical illnesses causing an acute alteration in the sensorium include: 1) CNS infections, such as meningitis and encephalitis; 2) intracerebral and intraventricular hemorrhage, hypertensive encephalopathy and head trauma; 3) metabolic derangements (i.e., uremic and hepatic encephalopathy, Reye's syndrome, hypoglycemia, hypercalcemia, hypernatremia, and hypokalemia); and 4) endocrine disorders including hyperthyroidism and diabetes mellitus.

COMPLICATIONS OF DRUGS OF ABUSE

Aspiration pneumonia is seen commonly with overdose from depressant drugs. Other pulmonary complications include pulmonary emboli, pulmonary edema (seen especially with narcotics), and pneumococcal pneumonia. Alcohol abuse may lead to a fatty liver, hepatitis, cirrhosis, gastrointestinal bleeding, gastritis, gastric ulcer, iron and folate deficiency, and bone marrow depression. Cutaneous bullae and necrotic ulcers are common with severe barbiturate overdose. Finally, intravenous use of drugs results in phlebitis, subacute bacterial endocarditis, septic arthritis, osteomyelitis, hepatitis and tetanus.

TREATMENT

Initial therapy for overdose of any abused drug involves prompt removal of the ingested product. In the alert patient, syrup of ipecac is the preferred method. In the obtunded or depressed patient, gastric lavage is used, with endotracheal intubation being reserved for the patient who has lost his gag reflex and is experiencing severe CNS depression. With the exception of alcohol, all abused drugs are effectively adsorbed by activated charcoal. Activated charcoal, given repeatedly every 6 to 8 hours, is also useful with anticholinergic agents. Finally, catharsis with magnesium sulfate will generally hasten removal of the ingested product from the gastrointestinal tract. Drugs causing decreased bowel motility and pooling in the gastrointestinal tract (for example, narcotics and anticholinergic agents) require particularly vigorous use of emesis or lavage, activated charcoal, and magnesium sulfate. Specific antidotes used include naloxone hydrochloride for narcotics, physostigmine for anticholinergic overdoses, and diphenhydramine for the extra-pyramidal tract effects seen with phenothiazines. A withdrawal syndrome may be associated with a prolonged high dosage of alcohol, opiates, barbiturates, and non-barbiturate hypnotics and are respectively treated with diazepam, methadone, short-acting barbiturates, and diazepam. Enhanced renal excretion of abused drugs may be accomplished with ionized diuresis. Alkalinization of the urine with sodium bicarbonate is effective with long-acting barbiturates. Acidification of the urine with ammonium chloride will result in enhanced excretion of amphetamines and phencyclidine. Psychotic reactions seen with hallucinogens, amphetamines, and phencyclidine are best treated with chlorpromazine or haloperidol while acute anxiety states respond well to benzodiazepines.

COMMON SIGNS AND SYMPTOMS, BIOCHEMICAL ABBERATIONS, AND THERAPY

Ethanol

Signs and symptoms resulting from the acute ingestion of ethanol include excitation, euphoria, and mild ataxia at low overdose, and coma at high overdose.[17] An ingestion of one ounce of 90 proof alcohol or one bottle of beer will raise the blood ethanol level twenty-five mg percent. Ethanol levels generally correlate in a predictable fashion with expected clinical signs and symptoms. Metabolic changes seen with ingestion of alcohol include lactic acidosis and ketosis, hypoglycemia, and hyperosmolarity.[11,17] Hypoglycemia does not occur when the ethanol level peaks, but 3 to 4 hours following ingestion. This contributes to coma and may produce seizures.

Hyperosmolarity found with ethanol overdose is of diagnostic and therapeutic value. A level of 100 mg% of ethanol will raise the serum osmolarity 25 mosm/kg, thereby serving as a rapid method for approximating the blood ethanol level. Ninety-five percent of an ingested dose of ethanol is removed from the body by hepatic metabolism resulting in removal of ethanol at a rate of 50 mg% per hour or 18 cc of 90 proof alcohol per hour.

Therapy involves prompt removal of the ingested ethanol if the patient is seen within 1 or 2 hours of ingestion. Activated charcoal is not effective and dialysis, while highly effective, is rarely needed. Further therapy includes correction of acidosis, institution of maintenance fluids, and attention to possible complications accompanying chronic ethanol use.

Barbiturates

Long-and short-acting barbiturates result in excitation, ataxia, and nystagmus in low overdose, and obtundation, coma, and respiratory depression in high overdose.[15] Pulmonary edema is also a common finding with overdose from short-acting barbiturates. Subcutaneous bullae are seen in severe poisoning cases. Therapy thereby requires prompt removal of the ingested product by emesis or lavage, gastrointestinal decontamination with activated charcoal, and catharsis. Subsequent barbiturate therapy requires consideration of its pharmacology. Short-acting barbiturates have a P_{ka} of 7.9 and the majority of an ingested dose is handled by hepatic metabolism. Long-acting barbiturates, on the other hand, have a lower P_{ka} (7.2) and are removed from the body both by hepatic metabolism and renal excretion. For long-acting barbiturates it is essential that acidosis be corrected promptly to prevent clinical worsening due to increased diffusion of the nonionized drug into the CNS. For the long-acting barbiturates, increased fluids, osmotic agents, and diuretics will all enhance renal excretion of the parent compound. In addition, alkalinization of the urine to a ph of greater than 7.5 (and preferably as close to 8 as possible) will result in significantly increased excretion of the barbiturate from the body. Finally, because of a prolonged long half-life in overdose and because long-acting barbiturates are moderately well dialyzed, hemodialysis or hemoperfusion should be considered for the most severe overdoses. For short-acting barbiturates, because increased fluids and ionized diuresis do not lead to increased excretion of the parent compound, maintenance fluids alone are indicated. Short-acting barbiturates are inadequately removed by hemodialysis. Consequently, a conservative approach to therapy is the best approach to management of the short-acting barbiturate.

Benzodiazepines

Valium, Librium, and Dalmane result in mild degrees of CNS depression. They are additive to other depressant drugs in causing obtundation and coma. Among drug ingestions reported to the Massachusetts Poison Information Center in 1978, Valium was only preceded in frequency by aspirin-containing compounds as a cause of drug ingestion.

Benzodiazepines are removed from the body entirely by hepatic metabolism. Consequently, therapy involves prompt removal of the ingested drug by emesis or lavage, use of activated charcoal, and gastrointestinal catharsis. Further management is supportive.

Phenothiazines

Phenothiazines cause variable states of CNS and respiratory depression and hypotension. Overdose management involves supportive therapy. Dystonic reacitons, generally occurring at therapeutic doses, manifest with opisthotonus, oculogyric crises, torticollis, and diffuse hypertonicity. All are alleviated with 50 mg intravenously of diphenhydramine given every 6 hours for a 24 hour period.

Inhalants

Inhalants, abused most commonly by the young adolescent, include glues, cements, and other volatile hydrocarbons. Clinical effects include euphoria and CNS excitation. Complications include sensatization of the myocardium leading to arrhythmias, hepatic and renal dysfunction, and bone marrow depression. Treatment includes removal of the patient from the site of exposure and careful monitoring of hepatic, renal, and marrow function.

Amphetamines

Amphetamines, taken either orally or intravenously, cause CNS stimulation leading to agitation and increased motor activity. Psychological effects include psychotic reactions, paranoid schizophrenic behavior, hallucinations, and intensification of anger and suspicion. The pupils are generally dilated. Chronic usage of amphetamines may result in cerebral vascular accidents.[10] Angiographic studies demonstrate segmental vessel constriction, and pathologic findings include cerebral hemorhage as well as thrombosis. Cardisvascular effects include hypertension and cardiac arrhythmias.

Amphetamines are weak bases with a P_{ka} of 10. The drugs are removed from the body by hepatic metabolism and renal excretion. Amphetamines have a moderate volume of distribution. Optimal therapy includes rapid removal of the ingested amphetamine by emesis or lavage, activated charcoal, and gastroinestinal catharsis. Enhanced excretion of the compounds may be accomplished by acidification of the urine to pH 4 to 5 with ammonium chloride at a dose of 2.75 meq kg intravenously every 6 hours.[8]

Excess motor agitation seen with amphetamines may be effectively treated with phenothiazines such as chlorpromazine and, as recently described, the butryophenones such as haloperidol and droperidol.[6,8] The latter two drugs appear to have strong antagonist action to amphetamine-induced CNS stimulation. Their use should be titrated against desired therapeutic effect.

Cocaine

Cocaine taken orally or by inhalation is a potent CNS stimulant resulting in excitation and seizures.[9] The drug is excreted predominantly by hepatic metabolism. Gastrointestinal decontamination and control of seizures are the major treatment considerations.

Narcotics

The narcotics, abused by the adolescent, involve a wide range of pharmaceutical agents including heroin, opium, propoxyphene, methadone, codeine, and pentazocine. Clinical findings include miotic pupils, and CNS and respiratory depression. Cardiac arrhythmias and seizures are infrequent complications of narcotic overdose. Heroin overdose often causes pulmonary edema and is also sometimes seen with methadone and propoxyphene.

Narcotics are distributed widely in body fluids and are present in low concentrations in the blood. They are removed from the body predominantly by hepatic metabolism. Therapy includes prompt removal of the narcotic from the gastrointestinal tract by emesis or lavage, adsorption by activated charcoal, and vigorous gastrointestinal catharsis. Since the drugs are handled entirely by hepatic metabolism and pulmonary edema is a potential risk, maintenance fluids alone are indicated. Naloxone hydrochloride is the specific narcotic antagonist of choice.[7] It results in reversal of hypotension, respiratory depression, miosis, and CNS depression. It acts by competitive antagonism with the ingested narcotic at receptor sites in the brain. The drug is given intravenously, 1.2 mg (3 ampules), with expected therapeutic response observed within 2 to 5 minutes of giving the drug. It may be repeated once if response does not occur. Lack of reversal of chemical signs suggests either that the diagnosis of the ingested narcotic was incorrect or that an inadequate dose of naloxone was given. Once an expected therapeutic response has been achieved, the drug should be continued either by continuous intravenous or repetitive bolus infusion. Because of the excellent therapeutic response and lack of adverse side effects, naloxone is the preferred method of therapy for narcotic overdose. Hemodialysis and hemoperfusion for narcotics is ineffective.

Phencyclidine

Abuse of phencyclidine has been widespread since 1970, and has nationwide use.[4,12,13] Easily synthesized in amateur laboratories and available under multiple names, it is popular among adolescents because of its pleasant effects. Its effects (in low dose) include euphoria, confusion, restlessness, agitation, constricted pupils, staring, horizontal and vertical nystagmus, and decreased corneal reflexes. In high doses, hallucinations, obtundation, coma, opisthotonus, hypertension, convulsions, arrhythmias, and CNS and respiratory depression are seen. Rhabdomyolysis has also been described. Tolerance develops with prolonged use of the drug.

Phencyclidine is a weak base, with a P_{ka} of 8.5. It is removed from the body by renal excretion as well as hepatic metabolism. It undergoes an enterogastric circulation with secretion of active drug into the stomach. Initial therapy involves prompt emesis or lavage, use of activated charcoal, and magnesium sulfate catharsis. Enhanced removal of the drug from the body can be accomplished by continuous nasogastric suction and acidification of the urine.[1] The former will remove phencyclidine secreted into the stomach. Acidification of the urine to a pH less than 5.0 with ammonium chloride via nasogastric tube (2.75 meq/kg every 6 hours) and Ascorbic acid given intravenously (2 gm every 6 hours) will increase the ionized fraction of the drug passing through the tubules, thereby limiting its reabsorption. These procedures should be reserved for more serious patients and should be continued until the patient's clinical state has returned to normal.

Anticholinergic Drugs

Commonly abused anticholinergic agents include tricyclic antidepressants, atropine and belladonna derivatives, antihistamines, and various plants.[18] Clinical findings in overdose include the following:

1. CNS
   - agitation
   - hallucinations
   - convulsions
   - coma
2. Autonomic nervous system
   - dilated pupils
   - dry mouth
   - hyperthermia
   - tachycardia
   - decreased bowel motility
   - urinary retention
3. Cardiovascular system
   - hypertension
   - hypotension
   - cardiac arrhythmias[14]

All anticholinergic drugs are well absorbed, have wide volumes of distribution in the body and are eliminated predominantly by hepatic metabolism.[2]

Treatment includes prompt removal with ipecac syrup or gastric lavage, if seen within 4 hours of ingestion, activated charcoal, and vigorous gastrointestinal catharsis with magnesium sulfate or citrate. Supportive care includes respiratory support, maintenance intravenous fluids, prompt correction of acidosis, plasma expanders for hypotension, catheterization for urinary retention, and anticonvulsant therapy. Physostigmine has a role in the reversal of CNS excitation or depression, anticholinergic manifestations, hypertension and cardiac arrhythmias.[14, 18] Hemodialysis and hemoperfusion are not effective for anticholinergic drugs.

REFERRAL AND FOLLOW-UP

The suicide attempt may be a pleas for help, a desire to manipulate the environment, or a personal expression of grief, guilt, or anger. Suicidal behavior is a result of impulsive handling of stress in an environment which is often neglectful or nonsupportive. This "acting out" behavior is especially common in the troubled adolescent and accounts for the high incidence of non-fatal suicidal attempts in this age group. All such adolescents are at risk of future self-injury and individualized therapeutic measures are essential to minimize this risk. Medical triage of these patients is facilitated by a careful, initial interview and categorization based on a distress and lethality scale.[5A] A small number of asymptomatic adolescents who have taken an overdose may be followed closely on an outpatient basis. The largest number of adolescents, whether asymptomatic or symptomatic, will require hospital admission. They generally do not require constant nursing observation but are helped by the opportunity to "cool off" in a protective environment. These individuals will require subsequent medical or psychiatric therapy.[15A] Finally, a small percentage will also require constant nursing observation with intensive psychiatric intervention.

Hospitalization on a pediatric service will provide supportive environment with close subsequent medical or psychiatric follow-up and be sufficient and appropriate for most suicide attempts. Only patients who are psychotic will require psychiatric admission and more intensive psychiatric intervention.

REFERENCES

1. **Aronow R, et al:** Phencyclidine overdose. JACEP *7(2)*:56, 1978
2. **Bickel MH:** Poisoning by tricyclic antidepressant drugs. Int J Clin Pharmacol 11 (2):145, 1975
3. **Bourne G:** Acute drug abuse. New York, Academic Press, 1976
4. **Burns RS, et al:** Phencyclidine deaths. JACEP 7(14):135, 1978
5. Diagnosis and management of reactions to drug abuse. Medical Letter 19(3):13, 1977

5A. **Curran, BE:** Suicide. Pediatr Clin North Am *26* (4):727–746, 1979

6. **Espelin DE, et al:** Amphetamine poisoning. N Engl J Med 278:1361, 1968
7. **Evans IEJ, et al:** Treatment of drug overdose with maxolone. Lancet 1:452, 1973

8. **Gary NE, et al:** Methamphetamine intoxication. Am J Med 64:537, 1978
9. **Gay GR, et al:** Cocaine in correct perspective. Anaesth Analg 55:582, 1976
10. **Hart JB, et al:** The adverse effects of amphetamines. Clin Toxicol 8(2):179, 1975
11. **Levy LJ, et al:** Ketoacidosis associated with alcoholism in non-diabetic subject. Ann Int Med 78:213, 1973
12. **Liden CB, et al:** Phencyclidine—nine cases of poisoning. JAMA 234:512, 1975
13. **Lundberg, JD, et al:** Phencyclidine. Clin Toxicol 9(4):503, 1976
14. **Manoguerra AS, et al:** Poisoning with tricyclic antidepressant drugs. Clin Toxicol 10(2):149, 1977
15. **Matthew H:** Barbiturates. Clin Toxicol 8(5):495, 1975

15A. **Marks, A:** Management of the suicidal adolescent on a non-psychiatric adolescent unit. J Pediatr 95:305–308, 1979

16. **Mitchell AA, et al:** Drug induced coma and pupillary constriction. Pediatr 89:303, 1976
17. **Robinson AB, et al:** Ethanol ingestion. N Engl Med 284:1253, 1971
18. **Rumack B:** Anticholinergic poisoning: treatment with physostigmine. Pediatrics 52:449, 1973
19. Survey by mayor's counsel on drug abuse. Boston, Ma 1978

five

managing the suicidal adolescent

William A. Long, Jr.

The threat of suicides occurring among a large group of teenagers in an Adolescent Medicine practice (limited to those 11 to 20 years of age) is ever present, and during certain seasons may appear daily in an overt or veiled form. To be true to formal training, it would perhaps be ideal to hospitalize each suspected case of potential suicide and seek the expert opinion of a psychiatrist. However, as every clinical practitioner must eventually face, the financial and time expenditures would be enormous, and rather quickly preclude a "suicide policy" in management or treatment of such cases. On the other hand, to take the risk of an adolescent's making sound judgments in the face of severe stress is a serious responsibility for any physician. Thus the dilemma: Should the physician take no chances and cover every suspicion, or should the physician develop methods or techniques to calculate that risk more accurately, thereby moderating the cost at minimal threat to the patient's life.

HANDLING THE VICTIM

Of course no one would quarrel with a totally thorough and studied approach to preventive care in such life-or-death situations. Therefore, the purpose is certainly not to condemn such conscientious coverage of potentially deadly circumstances. Rather, an investigation of a practical alternative applicable to clinical pediatrics is in order in light of the cold impracticalities of the ideal method.

A number of rationales are familiar in dealing with the suicidal adolescent. The fact that the patient in the hospital, under the tightest of security protection, might be successful in carrying out his fatal intent should be acknowledged. Close scrutiny will not last indefinitely in the life of a young patient. He or she might simply wait until the staff's vigilance is relaxed before completing his or her plan. These admitted facts certainly do not negate the previous ideal plan of management, but they do render it incorrectly named. Therefore, even a so-called "less-than-ideal" plan for universal hospitalization and psychiatric consultation leaves serious gaps which no one can always successfully circumvent. The attitude of assuming that any adolescent who even hints at suicidal thoughts must be referred will not be discussed. Better ways must be found to manage this fearsome problem.

Pediatricians should be alert to symptoms of psychotic behavior, and should be quick to admit that psychiatry is best equipped to handle such problems. This assumption thereby limits the discussion to the non-psychotic adolescent. Time should be available to give on demand, or practice schedules will be adjusted to carry through with counseling requirements, often imposed at inconvenient times. Suicidal crises are not scheduled events, and they must take priority over other items in the physician's long list of daily responsibilities. A relatively free hand should be ready in treating the teenage patient in question, even if his or her parents are not immediately available for consent. Most states will readily allow such emergency care without legal liability on the professional in charge.

The teenager who is contemplating suicide is feeling devoid of hope for improvement in the precipitating situation, mood, or circumstances, and feels that at least one of his or her practical alternatives is to end their earthly life. The teenager is feeling intolerably stressed by that situation or problem at hand, wants a way out of the critical depression and anxiety he is suffering and, in typical youthful fashion, wishes to find that escape route quickly. Complicating this desire for immediate relief are the distortions and fantasies he or she still holds concerning death itself. The teenager often disregards the fact that it is a terminal earthly event, and may even be considering the use of the suicidal act for double reward, providing respite from sufferings and perhaps gaining the affection, sympathy, and concern of family and peers, while avenging those who have offended or rejected with guilt. He or she will perhaps hold to the childlike philosophy of returning to life and function after allowing these events to produce their effects on those in his or her environment. Therefore, in this respect, suicide may be seen as a temporary measure.

With such pressing advantages apparent to the youth considering such a course, it is obvious that action on the part of the professional is a necessity. Attempts to gloss over the importance of even the most casual threat or statement concerning suicide are exceedingly risky. Intercessory professional action having then been established as a matter of the greatest importance, the physician should proceed to investigate approaches to the threatening non-psychotic teenager who has confided his or her plans or considerations to the physician.

Some observations concerning basic personality patterns, and the manner each of them relates to etiology and methodology of suicide can now be made. In so doing, some predictors will become apparent and these should assist in assessing the degree of risk in an individual and in setting a sensible approach and management plan.

A practical personality description would subdivide adolescents into four major categories: **aggressive independent, aggressive dependent, passive independent, and passive dependent.** The aggressive types are endowed with energy for taking overt action, while the passive individuals would be less prone to carry through with their threats, although not entirely immune from action. The independent types are categorically nonapproval-seeking, and would therefore be less concerned with the expectations and desires of others in their environment. On the other hand, the dependent individuals are much more aware of those expectations and more apt to comply with a management plan or more conscious of the negative aspects of a suicidal threat or act, whether or not it is successful.

Specifically, an aggressive independent adolescent, often impulse-ridden, endowed with poorly controlled energies (frequently diffusely directed), impatient to reach conclusions or find solutions, and possessing a poor self-image secondary to his many impulsive acts and offenses, is particularly prone to sudden rash suicidal attempts with little forethought. Many of these attempts, because of their violent or uncontrolled nature, are successful and often occur in the heat of a situational or emotional crisis, appearing to be almost accidental. The rescuer must be especially vigilant and must (if possible) anticipate circumstances which might precipitate an outburst that has terminal results. Such an impulsive youngster seems to profit greatly from the application of affectionate, firm, external controls which sometimes extend to even physical restraint. This harnesses his or her uncontrolled passions, while expressing deep personal concern. The advantages of a positive counseling relationship with this type of adolescent are numerous, especially when delineation of safe behavior limits, ego boosting, and attempts at improving self-image are primary goals.

On the other hand, the overachieving aggressive dependent youth may appear to be overcontrolled, hiding the despair and desperation he or she may be feeling in the face of adolescent ambivalence and the difficulty in expressing overt resentment and hostility. This type frequently turns these feelings upon self, and may become harshly perfectionistic and self-demanding, while developing growing fears of inadequacy and unworthiness. Youngsters in this group often take their lives without prior warning or symptoms after reaching a point where they find their suppressed feelings and depressed self-image to be intolerable. The anticipation of unexpressed ambivalence in all dependent adolescents may lead the therapist to the prevention of such tragedies. Open admission, in the presence of a sympathetic counselor, that the patient resents those who provide for and love him most will often release considerable tension. An earnest explanation to the teenager of the normalcy of this ambivalence might also be lifesaving.

The passive, independent teenager, often characterized as negative and stubbornly refusing to measure up to expectations, also runs a real risk of developing a low self-image as a result of poor performance in most areas (especially when pressured to perform by either parents or other authority figures). Despite a good intellect, he or she may repeatedly fall short in academic and social development, and without understanding the etiology of this underachievement, will often label himself or herself as being dumb, illiterate, and inadequate. Due to disappointment, guilt, and despair, this teenager will resort to suicide. The terminal act is often carefully planned, and it is often a successful one. However, suicidal threats without depression in this teenager are frequently experienced as a means of achieving a goal with parents, and also prove to be an effective means of gaining affection, protection, or privilege when there is open resentment and refusal to comply with parents' wishes. Again, a concerned counselor can do a great deal in helping these young patients recognize the destructive course they are pursuing, albeit a "personality game," and these insights with vigorous ego-boosting will usually interrupt their negative directions.

Passive dependent youngsters, most often compliant and "soft" in their actions, are probably least likely to commit suicidal acts so long as their potent dependency needs are satisfied. A loss to them, often in the form of estrangement from or rejection by a loved one may lead to an escape from this abandonment and loneliness. They might seek relief by terminating their miserable state through drug overdose. A compatible relationship with a counselor or other professional could well substitute for such a loss and thereby prevent such action.

Additional personality traits will add further interest and challenge to the prediction of suicide. For instance, an obsessive-compulsive youth who is likewise aggressive and impulse-ridden may be driven with an unrelenting desire to commit a violent act such as suicide. Such an additional trait in the aggressive over-controlled teenager may render him more perfectionistic, thereby all the more unable to achieve the ideals he strives for. This is all due to these unrealistic aims he sets for himself. This can lead to even more disappointment as he seeks his true identity, and the only recourse may seem to be self-destruction.

The hysterical child, fettered by self-dramatization, distortions of fact and concept, and exaggerated emotional responses, is perhaps the most prone to suicidal threats and gesturing. It is probably in this group that most of the unsuccessful suicide attempts occur. However, there are dangers present in any attempt and, accidental successes do occur in this group. Most of the gestures are fraught with a dramatic quality that demands the reaction of a party or parties toward whom this action is directed. Therefore, detection of the attempt becomes important. This is perhaps one of the chief reasons the success rate is quite low in this group of youngsters.

Phobic adolescents seem to be intent on self-preservation. Youngsters in this group use haring themselves as an absolute last resort, even in the face of terrible pressures. They will often retreat from frightening situations because they want to avoid discomfort or a specific threat.

This trait seems to have a protective quality about it, and may provied some considerable degree of immunity from suicidal thinking or action.

A careful evaluation of the individual youngster will help the physician or counselor to know what degree and type of immediate protection to afford the patient, what amount of effort to expend to develop a counseling relationship after initial rescue is assured, and what special risk factors to manage with direct action. Certainly by definition the suicidal adolescent, no matter what the personality structure, personal circumstances, peer or family relationships, or degree of achievement, is a lonely, despairing, hopeless, and sometimes desperate individual. This teenager has often abandoned even those resources that are available, whether they be physical, emotional, affectional, or spiritual. If there is a single factor which will act as the one most important preventive approach in such cases, it seems to be the extension of concern, reassurance, and loving control. These means can help the adolescent reconstruct a future plan for his or her life. A strong and supportive relationship can indeed be a lifesaving factor and is worth the careful attention and intense effort of all professionals who work with young people.

six
hospital treatment of the adolescent suicidal patient

Emmet M. Kenney and Kenneth J. Krajewski

Before beginning a discussion concerning treatment of adolescent suicide, the clinician must recognize the medical, social, and psychological impact of suicide. When reviewing statistics regarding the cause of death in American adolescents, the most common is accidents. Suicide is the second most frequent cause of death in the adolescent. Suicide is easily the more preventable cause of death.

When the question is raised as to the number of "accidents" that are in reality suicide, the health menacing nature of adolescent suicide grows to even greater catastrophic proportions. Adolescent suicide represents an area that requires a major investment by the medical community. Since approximately one in 200 adolescents will make a serious suicide attempt in some time of their adolescent years, effective medical intervention can produce outstanding assets for the health and well-being of the adolescent community.

The family, the school, and the community must bear and respond to societal implications of an adolescent suicide or suicide attempt. It is important to emphasize that the adult community has not only the right but a duty to provide and insist on involving the adolescent in treatment after a suicidal gesture or attempt. It is also important for the clinician to be aware of the significant psychological impact of suicide on the community.

An example of this was a 16-year-old young man who, upon arriving home and taking some laundry to the basement, found his uncle a suicide victim of self-inflicted shotgun wound. After this traumatic experience, the young man, T. R., began experiencing recurring frightful and terrifying dreams. His school performance and extra-curricular activities markedly decreased. Prior to the traumatic event, T. R. was a healthy and psychologically well-adjusted adolescent. T. R. and his mother discussed this with their family physician. Initial treatment was supportive care and an antidepressant medication. T. R's course remained unchanged and the frequency and severity of the terrifying dream continued. T. R. was referred by his family physician for psychiatric evaluation and treatment. After outpatient supportive psychotherapy and a clinical course of Imipramine, there was a resolution and return to the previous level of functioning. Therefore, the adolescent might not only experience the psychological impact of a suicide, but, in alarming proportions, might be a victim of a suicidal act. The clinician must be sensitive to the medical, social, and psychological nature of suicide.

THE PRESENTATION OF THE SUICIDAL ADOLESCENT

At times there is uncertainty in the medical community regarding the treatment of the suicidal adolescent. One view is the insistence of Doctor Thomas Szaz, widely read psychiatrist, who, in his opinion, states that adults have the right to suicide if they are not suffering from a major psychiatric illness. This complicates the decision-making ability of certain treatment personnel who extend Szaz's concern to patients of the adolescent years.

Another view is the adolescent's right to refuse treatment. This has resulted in hesitancy and at times confusion in the parental and medical response to the suicide gesture or attempt. Uncertainty may prevail in the community's and local authorities' response to the suicidal adolescent. However, recent supreme court and local district court decisions have clearly confirmed the parental right and the community right to treat adolescents who have psychiatric problems without regard to total voluntariness. Many in the medical community fail to see treatment as an extension of the parental rights and duties. It is the physician's personal opinion that the adolescent suicide attempt or gesture should always be treated as a cry for help and as evidence of at least moderate mental illness.

Physicians believe that the suicidal gesture in the adolescent is an adjustment reaction. The suicidal gesture is evidence of dangerousness to self. Therefore, when the adolescent presents to the medical community with evidence of mental illness and dangerousness to self, the medical community must respond with definitive care, and involuntary hospitalization may be necessary.

It is the physician's opinion that unless a patient is known extremely well psychiatrically to the physician who attends him in the emergency setting, the emergency room physician should recommend hospitalization for an evaluation of the suicidal adolescent patient. The first concern should be the acute life-saving maneuvers that may need to occur in the emergency room, if not beforehand, by the rescue squad who brought the patient in. This may involve resuscitation, trauma surgery, monitoring of the cardiovascular system, intubation, gastric lavage, etc. After the life-saving maneuvers have been accomplished, it becomes important that the individuals who serve the patient discuss with the parents and the adolescent the need of hospitalization preferably on a psychiatric pavilion designed for adolescents. Brief, short-term psychiatric hospitalization is superior to the patient being hospitalized in either a general medical or a pediatric ward. The following areas should be discussed:

1. Identifying the suicidal gesture as a cry for help
2. Identifying the suicidal gesture as need for special observation
3. Identifying the suicidal gesture as a need for immediate intervention
4. The need to identify the suicidal gesture as an indication that psychiatric intervention into the family process is mandator

There are advantages in having the youngster treated with others his own age by a staff with special sophistication in dealing with the adolescent years. It is important to remind the parents that they are free to visit the unit, and if they change their mind about treatment, they may sign their youngster out of the unit. The clinician must be supportive of the parental rights and duties, and that medical treatment is an extension of the parents' and society's rights and duties for the adolescent. Hospitalization is mandated whenever a suicidal gesture or attempt is made. The only exception would be when the individual is already under the care of an effective adolescent-experienced therapist since he may see the recent attempt or gesture as a means of re-entering a dependency-providing environment that the patient has already outgrown. If there is no psychiatric hospital pavilion available, anyone can get by with hospitalizing in a non-psychiatric general hospital unit if certain precautions are taken. Most hospitals have what they call **suicidal precautions** which include such things as making the environment safe by the removal of hazardous objects, by securing windows adequately, etc. Precautions also include constant observation by nursing personnel or family. In some cases, a less severe, but still effective method is that the patient will be left no more than momentarily out of nursing observation. This is difficult to arrange in all hospitals but can be accomplished. Phone calls should be limited to the parents only. It is important to reduce or eliminate the psychological payoff that exists so often in the adolescent suicide.

The structure of visitation including its limits (*i.e.*, initial visitation rights should be limited to parents or responsible guardians) must be established and monitored by the clinician. To exemplify the importance of the clinician's awareness and ability to respond to psychological payoff of many adolescent suicide attempts, the following case is described.

> Mary was a student at a local girl's school in a small midwestern city. After a suicide attempt, she was put in a general hospital ward. Teachers, students, and administrators of the school responded with warmth, empathy, and curiosity. Mary, who had been ignored throughout most of her school career suddenly found herself the center of attention. Cards were signed by the entire class, with classmates cutting school to spend time with her. It was rare when throughout the course of the day there weren't people from the school there. Within two weeks, six other girls of the same school made suicidal gestures. Hospitalization in a general ward became, psychologically, a very attractive thing to these adolescents. When the last three were transferred to the psychiatric pavilion where there were no visitors and no phone calls were permitted except from parents, the psychological payoff was removed and this series came to an abrupt halt.

Another example is the emergency room in a general hospital where it is fashionable and more or less routine for suicidal adolescents to be admitted into a pediatric ward. It is not uncommon to see two or three visitors (adolescents) spend time with the patient. Many of these youngsters were being given attention by people who didn't know they existed prior to the suicide attempt. They were in effect often treated as if they were very special friends or lovers. When the hospitalized adolescent was returned to the regular school atmosphere, they quickly drifted into the position of being ignored. The "hospital visitors" settled into their routine and the adolescent who attempted suicide experienced increasing frustration and increasing feelings of not belonging. This situation frequently results in reattempts or recurrence of suicidal gestures. The physician must use every suicidal attempt or gesture as a point to convey to the adolescent that suicide is a poor method of promoting change in their interaction with others.

SUICIDE AND THE SUICIDAL ADOLESCENT

The physician must realize that suicide is a response to a given stimulus. The ***stimulus*** that confronts the adolescent is accelerated. The time from puberty to early adulthood is a time of dramatic change in a relatively short period of time. It is a period of physical as well as social change. The social sphere of the adolescent mushrooms with increased interactions with others. Often, the adolescent suicide attempt or gesture is a ***response*** to the change in the social sphere. Many times, the suicide gesture or attempt is a ***method*** to promote change in the interactions with others. During adolescence there is a newness of both stimuli and responses. It is a time of first loves, where feelings and emotion are virginal and untested. In adolescence, the methods to deal with stress as well as to promote changes are untested. Many times the adolescent will be overwhelmed by the ineffectiveness of his responses and methods to deal with change in the face of accelerated growth.

Most adolescents have a rich fantasy world. Through the use of fantasy, many adolescents attempt to deal with untested methods and responses. One also sees adolescents employing fantasy to deal with failures they have experienced with ineffective responses. The suicidal adolescent will have a fantasy concerning death, possibly fantasizing that he will cause pain in the life of the family member or friends who have caused him real or imagined pain. The patient frequently goes through a funeral fantasy in which others sit around beating their breasts and saying, "If only I had it to do over again", or "Why didn't I treat him better", or "Why didn't I ever tell him (or her) that he(she) was a good son or daughter?"

It is our practice to aggressively confront the adolescent about this fantasy and to really test it. This can be accomplished in a variety of ways. If the adolescent is fairly sophisticated, the physician may have him read the portion of the book, "From Here to Eternity," where Corporal Bloom suicides. Bloom suicides with the full expectation that the men in his company will run in and claim great affection and feeling for him. Bloom envisions that his company will be angry at his rival for the attention of the group. The adolescent is surprised when they read that the shot which ended Bloom's life was met by Bloom's company with expletives decrying the fact that Bloom messed up the barracks right before inspection. It is imperative to use every suicidal attempt or gesture to establish the reality that suicide is a poor method to promote change. To confront the suicidal fantasy of the adolescent, the physician will often use case experiences of suicide victims. The physician will relate that relatives and friends of the suicidal patient will often protect themselves from any guilt by reassuring themselves that they did everything they could for their departed relative by depreciating the suicide victim. We describe the patronizing statements made in such occasions as, "Well, Lord knows we tried," and "Maybe he or she is better off." We also attempt to describe in detail people who have repeatedly attempted suicide. We describe how the individual's response to the suicide attempt becomes progressively less intense with each attempt. The suicidally-proned individual will become more dramatic and more severe with each attempt. The last message to someone who repeatedly uses suicide as a method of controlling love objects is, "Who cares" or "You haven't got the guts", which often forces the patient to go out and commit the final act. From the previous discussion and examples, it should be apparent that the physician should discuss suicide, suicide impulses, and suicide consequences with the adolescent patient in almost every psychotherapeutic encounter. In fact, if suicidal thoughts and impulses have been a problem, the physician should start daily psychotherapy sessions with the patient by asking about the presence of these particular symptoms.

In any discussion of suicide three levels can be discerned concerning the suicide patient. The first level is the patient who has suicidal thoughts, and impulses. It is a fair statement that almost everyone has experienced a suicidal fantasy sometime in their life. This phenomenon is more common in early adolescence, but can occur at any time in an adolescent's life. It is not as serious as many people believe. Although teenagers are frequently at war with their environment and with their parents, they tend to idealize power.

The second level must emphasize the certain consequences of a suicidal attempt that the parents are impotent to do anything about. The physician should describe with examples the loss of function related to decrease of oxygenation during a suicidal attempt with barbiturates. The physician should discuss the loss of function with nerve injury in a wrist cutting. It should be emphasized that neither the parents nor the medical community can guarantee to completely undo the results of an attempted suicide. It comes as a surprise to many adults to learn that adolescents have an exaggerated opinion of the adult's capability of undoing their efforts.

The third level is the object of the suicidal maneuver and what movement is expected on the part of these love objects. For example, many adolescents who have violated certain parental rules will use a suicidal gesture as a "punishment maneuver" in an attempt to distract the parents from following through with their punishment. The psychiatrist makes a special effort to determine whether the youngster is somewhat hedonistic and feels he should not have to endure normal punishment or whether the parental punishment response is exaggerated. Another commonly experienced object of the suicide gesture or attempt is the peer group. One of the principle methods of leadership in the adolescent groups is to temporarily eliminate one of the weakest or least effective members from group participation by someone who is vying for a leadership position. If victimized by this leadership maneuver of "odd man out", the adolescent experiences a loss of status within the peer group. Some will respond to this maneuver with a suicide gesture or attempt. In therapy, the physician should point out that this is a leadership style and it is temporary. The physician should emphasize the presence of better methods of solving the problem. Besides the family and the peer group, a frequently encountered object of the suicide attempt or gesture is either a disappointment or a controlling maneuver in a romance. This can be tested according to its ineffectiveness as a permanent problem solving technique.

EVALUATION OF DEPRESSION IN THE ADOLESCENT

Depression can be classified into two broad categories, endogenous and exogenous. Endogenous depressions are biochemical in nature and therefore will show a significant response to antidepressant medication, such as tricyclic antidepressants or the monamine oxidase inhibitors. Manic-depression is an endogenous depression. Exogenous depression is external in nature and shows very little response to antidepressant medication. In an exogenous depression, antidepressants might produce some beneficial effects mainly through their anxiolytic and sedative properties. However, the use of antidepressants for these effects are not recommended. Neuroses, depressed type, and situational depressions are examples of exogenous depressions. The typical adolescent depression is exogenous in nature. (The literature has very few references of endogenous depression in adolescents.) This is not to say that an adolescent cannot become endogenously depressed. We have seen endogenously depressed adolescents and there is definite evidence that this illness is increasing in numbers in the population. During hospitalization, it is the physician's intent to look for evidence of a severe depression. Accurate and thorough evaluation of depression in the adolescent is the foundation of treatment and hospital management.

The adolescent's typical sleep pattern is one in which he or she does not want to get up in the morning and has difficulty going to bed at night. Thus, when a teenager is severely depressed, one sees a dramatic reversal in the previously mentioned pattern. During morning rounds, the nursing staff will report that the patient went to bed early or that the patient has been up and asking for permission to be out of his room or attempting to pace the halls early in the morning. Another significant vegetative sign is loss of appetite, which is different than what other adolescents experience. The severely depressed adolescent loses interest in food rather than becoming a little fussier about what they eat. Self-depreciation and self-worthlessness can be fairly pronounced in a severe depression. It is important to recognize a maneuver that is employed which can be mistaken for self-depreciation. This can be encountered when physicians are examining residents in a mock board situation. At regular intervals, certain residents would come in and look like they were suffering from self-depreciation. Certain residents would state that they were not particularly good residents, and the physicians' natural response was to reassure them that they were valuable and effective. Once the physicians spotted the maneuver and challenged it by agreeing with the self-depreciating statement, the residents were quickly able to come to their own defense. The same is true in adolescents who use this pseudo self-depreciation as a maneuver to extract support, so in an interview they may say such things like, "Well, I'm not a very good son," or "I'm not as effective as other people my age," or, "I have disappointed people." If the therapist plays the devil's advocate and accepts at face value these statements, as if they were true, he may find that the patient in effect denies a severe depression by coming to his own defense. During hospitalization, the physician can monitor in detail the adolescent's self image when dealing with nursing and ancillary staff, as well as other adolescents on the unit. If the adolescent is severely depressed, there is an impairment in the ability to fight. Self-condemnation or the need to punish oneself is found in severe depression. The depressed individual usually doesn't defend himself in either group or individual interactions. The adolescent unit has emphasis on group therapy and interactions which makes it a good place to study the interaction of the patient with his peer group. Most healthy adolescents have a competitive drive. Using the gymnasium, classroom, and other leisure time activities, the physician has a good base to study the competitive efforts of the adolescent, and thus evaluate the severity of the depressive phenomena. It is important to assess the ability of the adolescent to express thoughts and feelings. Severely depressed individuals have decreased energy in expressing thoughts and feelings. One must be sensitive to this in that a severely depressed adolescent may appear to present very little emotional content or conflict, however internally and unverbalized, there may be considerable interpsychic turmoil. Support, empathy, and patience is a definite prerequisite of the treating physician.

A few words of caution must be expressed at this time when dealing with an evaluation of depression in an adolescent. When using the previously mentioned parameters for measuring the degree of depression, the clinician must keep in mind the degree of change with respect to time. A large degree of change over a considerable period of time could be totally benign in nature. However, a moderate degree of change over a brief period of time could represent a profound degree of depression. The degree or quantity of change must be measured over the period of time that this change takes place. The clinician must also be aware of the degree of change that the person is experiencing in relation to their own previous functioning and skills. An example can aid with this concept.

> Johnny was a very bright, gifted, and effective high school student who was involved in school activities such as student government and varsity sports. Within a month, he discontinued all school activities and his grades had dropped to slightly above average. Though he was still a cooperative student and above average as well as being well liked by others, he was experiencing a severe depressive phenonmenon. Without adequate assessment of the degree of functioning and the degree of change in time, the profound nature of his depression could be underestimated by the unskilled clinician.

In the evaluation of depression in the hospitalized adolescent, the clinician must be alert to the behavior of the severely depressed adolescent. Unlike an "acting out" adolescent, the severely depressed adolescent is complacent. Attention-seeking patterns and maneuvers are immobilized by the severity of the depression. The severely depressed adolescent's complacency will probably not mobilize the attention of the hospital staff when compared to the attention mobilized by an "acting out" adolescent. Complacency might be underestimated and the patient may be described as cooperative and well-behaved, which to some might be mistakenly interpreted as a lack of intrapsychic turmoil and conflict. The withdrawal and immobilization of a severe depression can by its very mechanism promote distance and withdrawal of attention by the helpers, and hinder evaluation as well as therapy.

CHEMOTHERAPY AND THE HOSPITALIZED ADOLESCENT

The role of antidepressants in the life of the endogenously depressed adult is a very important one, but the role of antidepressants in adolescents is usually exaggerated in the mind of most therapists. Since adolescents do not get endogenously depressed with any frequency, the vast majority of depressed adolescents will not respond to antidepressant medication. The individual who is depressed because of a neurosis will, of course, respond to the antianxiety effects of many of the tranquilizers. Short-term, low doses of major tranquilizers seem to be the drug of choice by many physicians in dealing with anxiety. Physicians tend to avoid minor tranquilizers in adolescent neurosis because it is important to have the adolescent learn alternative methods of dealing with anxiety than just experiencing it. The use of potentially habitual medications that can produce euphoria does not lend itself effectively as an adjunctive agent in intensive psychotherapy. Adolescent neurosis requires intensive psychotherapy. The short-term and limited use of major tranquilizers, with their non-addictive, non-euphoric qualities is an effective adjunct in intensive psychotherapy. The situationally depressed adolescent seldom needs medication over any great period of time. The only exception is the case of the impulse ridden individual, who might benefit from the major tranquilizers' dampening effect on certain impulsive responses. If there is clinical evidence of an endogenous, biochemically-related depression then antidepressant medications should be employed and titrated to a therapeutic level.

In evaluating any suicidal gesture or act, the clinician must be able to evaluate not only the depressive features but also the presence of any psychotic symptomatology. The suicidal gesture or act can be the result of a psychosis. If after evaluation by a skilled psychiatrist it is found that the adolescent is experiencing psychosis, then therapeutic quantities and levels of antipsychotic agents must be employed. A short case presentation will exemplify this point.

> Jerry was a 16-year-old boy, whose grades dropped from A's to C's over a three month period. The family related that Jerry spent considerable time by himself and when he was involved with the family he was angry and hostile unlike his usual pleasant self. Jerry began talking of unusual powers and of hurting himself. On one occasion, he drove the family car 600 miles before abandoning it at the side of an interstate. Jerry was seen by his physician and it was felt that Jerry was experiencing an adjustment reaction. Subsequent to this Jerry left a suicide note and again took the family car. This time Jerry was involved in a head-on crash which was his fault. Fortunately no one was hurt. After being retained by legal authorities, Jerry was examined by a psychiatrist and found to have a thought disorder with a delusional system. Major tranquilizers were strongly indicated as well as acute psychiatric hospitalization.

Any suicide gesture or act should require a comprehensive evaluation not only for depressive features but also for psychotic features. If psychosis is present, a full course of antipsychotic chemotherapy is indicated as well as hospitalization on an adolescent psychiatric unit.

FAMILY AND FRIENDS OF THE HOSPITALIZED ADOLESCENT

In the hospital treatment of suicidal adolescents, the family's involvement in the treatment effort is one of paramount importance. Family involvement with the hospitalized adolescent should begin early in the course of treatment. If admission is through the emergency room, a conference is held with the psychiatric supervisor and the family to aid with the admission of adolescent to the hospital and to have the family involved with the treatment effort. When the adolescent is admitted to the unit, there is an in-depth interview with the parents and the youngster, partially together and partially separated. This material is used along with input of the attending physician to determine an early treatment plan. Social workers and social services are involved with the patient and family. On one evening a week there is a family group for the parents of the hospitalized adolescent where they are usually very responsive. The physician must be aware and sensitive to the family's emotional state surrounding the adolescent's suicide gesture or act. It is important to avoid scapegoating family members and also to avoid assigning responsibility for the suicide episode.

The treatment unit of the child is the family. The physician should inform parents that it takes seven to ten days to evaluate an adolescent fully and the vast majority of adolescent admissions are ready for either transitional or outpatient family therapy at the end of that time. It is important to keep the hospitalization period short with the adolescent. If the clinical situation warrants and it is necessary to prolong the hospitalization, it is important to increase family involvement and to have the family actively involved with decisions regarding hospital stay and visitation. If the suicidal adolescent has in fact been a source of frustration and pain to the parents prior to the suicidal gesture, an even moderate length stay is indicated in which parents are allowed to stay outside of the treatment program. This may result in a regrouping of the adolescent with the family by allowing the parents sufficient time to regroup the adolescent into the family unit. It is important to reiterate that severe placement complications can be avoided by having the family involved throughout the hospital stay. With familial involvement in the treatment effort there is far less difficulty re-integrating the adolescent into the family unit.

There are varying opinions concerning the role of adolescent visitors, as discussed previously in this chapter. It is our experience that adolescent visitors should not be allowed on an adolescent unit. The relationships of the adolescent with their friends can be used as a motivational stimulus to enter into the treatment program which allows them to rejoin the family before they rejoin their friendships. Romance does not need to be part of the adolescent treatment program. Phone calls or visits from girlfriends or boyfriends are not permitted. The treatment response in adolescents is far greater when there is a proper attitude of limitation on this particular visiting behavior. In limiting visitations it must be made clear that the hospital is a setting where one's efforts should be directed to find better problem solving techniques than suicide.

The suicide attempt or gesture not only involves the individual—it involves the family. The experienced therapist may need to warn the parents that the youngster who would try to mobilize guilt in the parents through a suicidal maneuver is also likely to use guilt promotion as a method of extracting himself from the hospital. This type of youngster frequently reports callousness or cruelty on the part of the nursing staff. Often this individual will indicate that the therapist is not willing or available to talk to him. Frequently, they describe all other patients on the unit as prostitutes and drug users. Reminding the parents of these frequently occurring statements as well as the maneuver they represent will protect the parents from the guilt the youngsters want to promote. This case will exemplify this point:

> Charlie was 15-years-old and, following a suicide gesture, accused the doctor of not wishing to talk to him. The doctor pointed out that he regularly made rounds and when he asked the youth to join in communication with him the youngster refused. Charlie's father subsequently approached the doctor and

stated that the doctor didn't understand that when he was making rounds in the morning his son did not like to get up. However, if the doctor would be so good as to come around in the afternoon his son might feel more like talking and be more receptive. When the physician hears this kind of response from a parent, the reason the youngster has put the parent into a bind is obvious.

There are parents who are willing victims to the controlling efforts of their children. During hospitalization the physician can effectively stabilize and rejoin the suicidal adolescent in to the family unit. It is important to realize the relationship of the suicidal adolescent to the family. As previously stated, the suicidal gesture or attempt is an ineffective means of promoting change in interpersonal relationships. However, through hospitalization the physician is allowed greater intervention to stabilize and rejoin the family unit.

Psychiatric hospital treatment is the treatment of choice for the suicidal adolescent. Through hospitalization, the family can be involved more effectively in the treatment program. The youngster will be seen daily by the attending psychiatrist. There is 24-hour observation of the adolescent's behavior including observation of dietary and sleeping habits. It is well established that parents are poor observers of the behavior of suicidal adolescents. Through hospitalization the clinician can more accurately assess the youngster's social skills and response to boys and girls of the same age. The response of the adolescent to authority figures as well as the response to group activities can aid in evaluation and treatment. During hospitalization the youngster can be involved with occupational and recreational therapy. Most modern psychiatric hospitals have their own classrooms with small group teaching designed to return the youngster to his environment. The educational therapist becomes an ally in returning the youngster to his appropriate classroom. The qualified educational therapist acts as the intermediary between the school system and the patient. If necessary, through conferences with school professionals, the schools can be more informed and involved with the youth's re-entry into the school system. With increased school involvement there is a more relaxed and structured re-entry of the adolescent.

THE SUICIDE GESTURE

As previously stated, the suicide gesture may be a maneuver to control or change interpersonal relationships. It is important to explore and confront these ineffective patterns. Some of the frequently encountered maneuvers of a suicide gesture will be seen here. The patient may not be willing to accept a parental decision about limitation of activities and will use the suicide gesture as a scare maneuver to open permission for certain activities. The second maneuver is an attempt to obviate punishment through a suicide gesture. The suicide gesture may be an anger response in an attempt to punish others. The response might be a reply to difficulty with peer group relationships. The gesture may be an attempt to move a special teacher, counselor, or therapist involved in ongoing therapy. It is important to identify the nature and significance of the relationship that the suicide gesture is directed toward.

During the hospital stay, the physician must involve the youngster in the stated objectives of keeping the patient alive as well as finding alternative methods for promoting change in interpersonal relationships. The physician must describe that the principal responsibility of the patient is to keep himself alive. The suicide rate is lower if the patient is handed the responsibility of reporting suicide impulses and thoughts to the psychiatric staff. Likewise, it is important to explain to the adolescent the responsibility and willingness of the staff and therapist to work with the youth in maintaining his health and well-being. A partnership between the patient and the therapeutic team will significantly reduce the suicide risk. It is important for the therapist to realize that up until the very last second the suicidal individual is ambivalent about the suicidal act as a means to solve a problem.

SUICIDE AND THE COMMUNITY

A number of years ago a study of depression was attempted in different adolescent populations. Depressive scales were used for rating randomly-selected students in a variety of high schools. The school selected represented a variety of social and cultural variables. The first school was a local technical school which served the ghetto and more deprived areas of the community. The second school was a private, all male, Jesuit prep school. The third school was an affluent suburban community high school. The fourth school was a high school serving the Air Force, with the dislocation problems of being an Air Force officer or enlisted man's child. The fifth was for a state reformatory's population. It had been predicted that the private school and the wealthy suburban school students would be similar in characteristics. It was also anticipated that dislocation problems of being career military persons offspring would increase depression and suicide. The results obtained provided some interesting results. The technical school which served the impoverished area did not have any higher depressive rating scale than most of the other schools involved. The private school and the wealthy suburban school differed to a marked degree. The school serving the military did not have as high a depressed rating as was anticipated. The youngsters in the reformatory had the highest depressive scale, which was anticipated. The second highest depressive scale was the wealthy suburban school. In an effort to determine a reason for the difference between the results of the suburban affluent school and the private school, a retrospective study was found that illuminated the differences between these schools. In the private school, parents invested money out of their own pocket for tuition as well as investing their own time and energy in being involved with the school and the educational process. Both the suburban school parents as well as the private school parents placed high expectations on their children. However, the parents of the affluent suburban community high school invested relatively little of their own time or energy into the educational process. It appears that with regards to different populations of students, the greater the parental involvement the smaller the depressive scale rating. Parent populations that invested less time and energy into the school system had school populations with increasing depressive scales that were proportionate to the parental involvement. The less parental involvement the greater the depressive rating. It is believed that increased community involvement with the adolescent produces reduction in depression.

The statistics of adolescent suicide demand the attention and intervention of the physician. Approximately 75 percent of all suicide victims see a physician within a four month period prior to the suicidal act. Eighty percent of those that commit suicide have attempted suicide at least one time previously. It is believed that the suicide attempt or gesture represents at least the presence of an adjustment reaction of adolescence as well as evidence of dangerousness to oneself or others. The suicide attempt or gesture in the adolescent requires careful psychiatric evaluation and aggressive treatment. This mandate of the medical community to care for the well-being of the adolescent is believed to be best accomplished (most effectively) through hospitalization in an adolescent psychiatric unit. With careful evaluation and treatment, a major cause of death in the adolescent population can be greatly reduced.

seven

suicide attempts and gestures: the poison center perspective

R. W. Moriarty, M.D.

The Pittsburgh Poison Center has had a long standing interest in the social and emotional aspects of poisonings. As evidence of this interest, the center was probably the first poison center in this country to employ a full time social worker.

In the fall of 1976, the Center became increasingly concerned about the number of suicide attempts and gestures in young children and adolescents that were being reported to the Center. In order to gain a better understanding of this problem and to improve the recognition and management of such cases, a study was undertaken.

For the purpose of the study, all cases of suicide attempts and gestures were reviewed. A *suicide attempt* was and continues to be defined as *a case of a purposeful exposure to any material with the clear intent of achieving bodily harm*. A gesture, while similar to an attempt in terms of the event, differs in terms of intent. With a gesture, the desire for bodily harm is less clear or entirely missing. However, due to the circumstances surrounding the case, the event cannot be classified as accidental. Cases of suicides were excluded from the studies since clearly these cases were beyond help. Furthermore, the study was confined to a review of cases involving patients 7 through 18 years of age. This group was chosen in the belief that if new management modes were uncovered they might be more successfully instituted in a younger age group.

The study period was from January, 1975 through June, 1976.

During that time the Pittsburgh Poison Center managed a total of 2,851 cases of exposures in the 7 to 18-year-old age group. Of this group, cases of attempted suicide accounted for 47 or 1.6 percent of the total group. Of these patients, 98 percent were age 13 years or older. The 215 cases of gestures equated to 7.5% of the total group. Again more than 90 percent of these cases occurred in the 13 to 18-year-olds. The almost five to one ratio of gestures to suicides may be due in part to reporting bias. Apart from the need for an interpretation of the intent of the action in the case, it is probably easier to classify a case as a gesture rather than as a suicide attempt, especially in the younger patient. Combined, the two modes of exposures accounted for 9.2 percent of the total group.

The sex ratio of the combined group was equal in the 7 to 12-year-old group. However, this ratio changed dramatically in the 13 to 15-year-olds. Here the ratio was seven females to one male. In the 16 to 18-year-old group, the ratio fell to three to one. For the group as a whole, the ratio was four females to one male. This was an interesting finding since non-suicide exposures in the same age groups tend to show a predominance of males. These results also supported the observation that the more physical type of suicide acts (*i.e.*, shooting, hanging, cutting) are primarily a masculine phenomenon. More than 99 percent of the cases involved an ingestion—at times often multiple. Inhalations occurred in less than one percent of the cases.

Drugs constitute the majority of the materials ingested. Household products were infrequently used. Again, there could be a bias in classifying this type of ingestion as a suicide attempt or gesture. The groups of drugs primarily involved included analgesics, tranquilizers and sedatives.

One of the more disturbing findings was that only 35 percent of the total group was referred to a member hospital of the Pittsburgh Poison Center system for further treatment and evaluation. Of those referred, only 13 percent were admitted.

These and other findings seemed to reflect a number of interrelated problems. There was concern that the index of suspicion regarding suicide attempts and gestures might be low among the Pittsburgh Poison Center staff. This could be particularly true with the younger patients. If this were the case, a partial solution might lie in developing an in-house education program designed to increase the awareness of our poison center staff. A measure of success of such a program would be an increase in the incidence of reporting such cases. If indeed there was under-reporting of these cases, part of the problem might be also due to the fact that there seemed to be a general negative attitude among many of the member hospital's emergency room staffs regarding the patient attempting suicide. This attitude was further complicated by the lack of appropriate referral facilities for such patients. Thus it was conceivable that our staff felt that there was little to be gained by referring such patients who were not overtly ill due to their ingestion to our member hospitals. The solution to this problem lies in developing programs for our member hospitals that encourages them to provide more "reasonable" management of these patients. In the fall of 1976 these various educational programs were instituted by the Pittsburgh Poison Center.

In September of 1978, a study similar to the previous one was undertaken to determine the impact of these programs. However, a decision was made to expand the study. In January of 1978, the National Poison Center Network (NPCN), which has the Pittsburgh Poison Center as its headquarters, began to institute a uniform data collecting system among its member centers. Due to the volume of cases being reported through this data system, it was felt that a review of all cases of suicide attempts and gestures might yield more representative information. For the first six months of 1978, data was collected on a total of 49,912 cases. This figure represents the case load of only 22 of the present 50 NPCN Centers, since the remaining centers did not begin to report until later in that time period. While the review of this data showed many of the trends previously observed, there were some interesting differences. The incidence of cases of suicide attempts and gestures had increased. About 20.3 percent of the NPCN cases of exposures that occurred in the 7 to 18-year-old group were placed into these categories as compared to the 9.2 percent observed in the previous study. Of this 20 percent, approximately 15 percent of the cases were gestures (compared to the previously reported figure of 7.5 percent) and 5 percent were suicide attempts as compared to the previous 1.6 percent. The Pittsburgh reporting rate of such cases rose from 9.2 percent to 19.7 percent. Both types of cases showed a gradual increase in incidence in patients age 7 to 11. At age 12 there was a dramatic increase in the number of cases of gestures with a peaking occurring at ages 15 to 16 years. Suicide at-

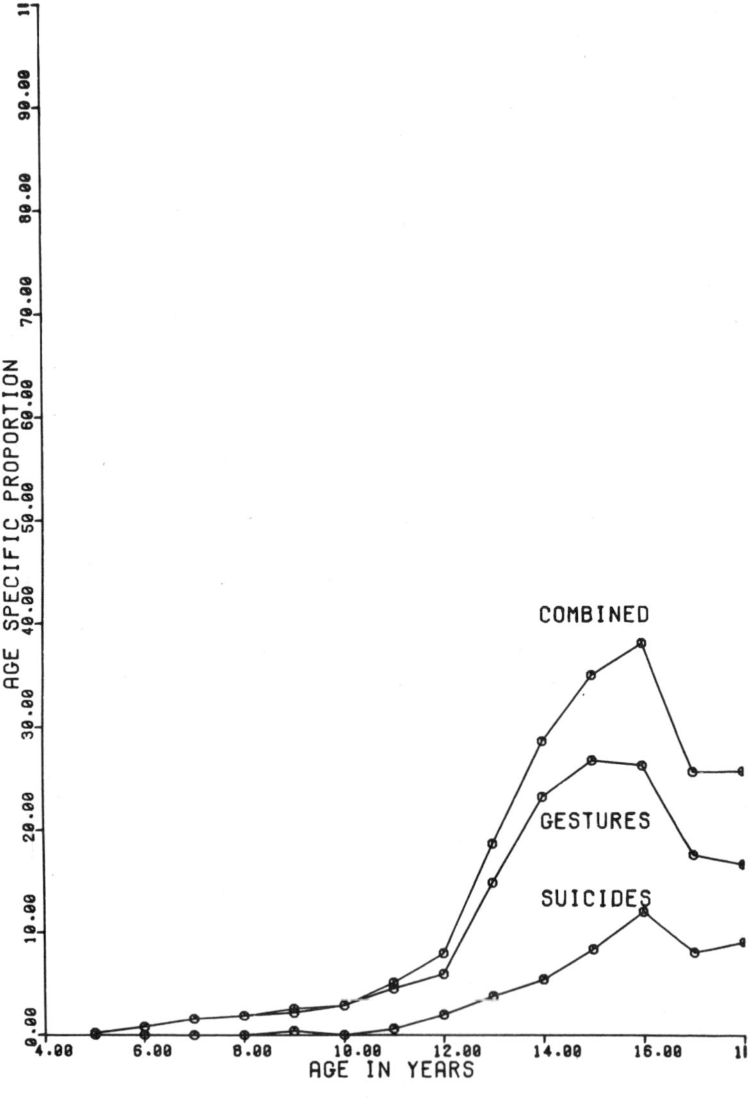

Fig. 7-1. Suicide and Attempts in Children and Youth
Age specific adolescent gesture and suicide rates based on combined 1978 National Poison Center Network data.

tempts also increased during the same ages but not as dramatically. These cases tended to peak at 16 years (See Fig. 7–1).

Females continued to predominate in both types of cases, although the sex ratio for the total NPCN group was 2.5 females to one male as compared to the previously observed ratio of four to one.

Drugs continue to be the primary agent of choice. Of the drugs ingested, five groups, namely, analgesics, tranquilizers, sedatives, antihistamines and antidepressants accounted for the majority of cases.

A study of the management of these cases revealed the most dramatic changes. For the total NPCN group, 65 percent of the cases were referred to an emergency room for further evaluation and treatment as compared to 35 percent in the previous study. Of those referred, 46 percent were admitted in contrast to the previous figure of 13 percent. A separate review of the Pittsburgh case management experience for both groups showed a doubling of the referral rate and a greater than four-fold increase in admissions over the previous study.

Detailing the management of the cases of suicide attempts, the NPCN study showed that 82 percent of these cases were referred for further treatment and evaluation; of this group, 46 percent were admitted. For the Pittsburgh group, 88 percent of these cases were referred; of that group, 75 percent were admitted. It would appear that either our educational efforts in Pittsburgh are succeeding or that we are catching up with the rest of the NPCN centers.

Management of these cases by the staffs of the poison center and the referral hospitals must be reviewed. If found to be inadequate, improvement can be obtained through diligent educational efforts. However, the question of whether or not such improved case finding and management techniques can significantly alter the final outcome in these patients has yet to be answered.

index

Page number followed by an f indicates reference to a figure; page number followed by a t indicates tabular material.